Transliteration:
Show Me the English

Transliteration:
Show Me the English

Jean Elaine Kelly

RID Press
Registry of Interpreters for the Deaf, Inc.
333 Commerce Street
Alexandria, VA 22314   USA
(703) 838-0030 V, (703) 838-0459 TTY
www.rid.org

Registry of Interpreters for the Deaf, Inc.

The Registry of Interpreters for the Deaf, Inc. (RID) is the only national organization of professionals who provide sign language interpreting/transliterating services for Deaf and Hard of Hearing persons. Established in 1964 and incorporated in 1973, RID is a tax-exempt 501(c)(3) non-profit organization.

RID has worked diligently to provide the "three Q's of interpreting: Quantity, Qualifications, and Quality," namely, the RID Triad. RID's Triad is composed of

- Training for new and professional Interpreters through the Certification Maintenance Program (CMP)

- Continued certification through RID's National Testing System (NTS)

- Self-regulation through a national Ethical Practices System (EPS)

RID Press is a division of the Registry of Interpreters for the Deaf, Inc., 333 Commerce Street, Alexandria VA 22314, USA, (703) 838-0030 V, (703) 838-0459 TTY, (703) 838-0454 Fax.

Published 2001

Internet: www.rid.org

Library of Congress Catalog Card Number: 2001-132112

ISBN 0-916883-32-9

Printed in the United States of America

■■ CONTENTS

■■■ ACKNOWLEDGEMENTS

It would be impossible to acknowledge all the people that have helped me learn how to become a transliterator; however, I want to credit the following people who, through their support and encouragement, were instrumental in helping me put this book together.

I want to first thank two special people in my life. The first is Elizabeth Mendoza for her encouragement, her guidance, and her willingness to work with me through this book

The second is my husband, Ian, who constantly encouraged me. You and the boys, Andrew and Eric, were very supportive, and I thank you all.

I would like to thank Barbara Neal Varma who started me analyzing the task of transliterating, the 1999 summer class that let me experiment with them, and Myrna Tenebaum, who helped with the beginning editing.

Specifically I want to thank the following people for their help: Jenna Cassel, Judy Viera, Wendy McNair, and Angela Jones.

■■ PREFACE

The information in this book is based on how transliterators use an English-based sign language for Deaf adults. This book is not intended to be used in any way to teach Deaf children English. Whether sign language interpreters interpret or transliterate, the decision should not be based on the wants of the interpreter, but rather, on the consumer's wants.

Since the 1970s, there has been a growing number of Interpreting Preparation Programs (IPPs) across the country set up for sign language interpreters. The focus of these programs has been to teach American Sign Language (ASL) and to train students how to interpret from ASL to English and English to ASL.

The task of transliterating does not get as much attention as the task of interpreting in most IPPs. In a survey of IPPs across the United States, it was found that out of 25 schools teaching interpreting, all but 2 teach transliterating skills. Of the remaining 23 programs, 10 teach transliterating skills for less than 50% of the time during one interpreting class, and 13 programs have only one class in which they teach transliterating (Kelly, 1999).

With only 2 years in most IPPs, the feeling is that class time spent on teaching transliterating is wasted, as this is a skill that will be easily acquired once the student learns how to interpret. A common belief among many educators and sign language interpreters is that once an individual has learned ASL-to-English and English-to-ASL interpretation, then English-based transliteration should not be a problem. If transliteration merely requires the interpreter to follow English, just how hard can it be? As a profession, we have found out just how hard. In 1989 the Registry of Interpreters for the Deaf (RID), a non-profit organization that has been testing and certifying interpreters since 1972, divided the task of interpreting and transliterating into two separate performance tests, where before there had only been one test. In the first 4 years the two performance tests were offered, the failure rate for the Certificate of Transliterating (CT) was almost 54%, while the failure rate for the Certificate of Interpreting (CI) was 27% (Personal correspondence with RID National Office, 1999).

When I started interpreting in 1973, I was often asked by Deaf consumers to "show me the English." Through their patience and tutelage, I learned what they meant. I was truly dependent on the consumer's wants, as there were no books, training, or videos to show me. I eventually discovered that what I was doing was transliterating. Later, I began to observe other interpreters and question consumers to try to understand what the task of transliterating entailed. Throughout the years I have worked on improving my transliterating skills and mentored others in the field who wanted to improve their transliterating skills. This book is an attempt to share this information with others by providing a simple and easy way to teach the building blocks of transliterating.

This book was set up with two goals in mind. The primary goal is to have a standardized curriculum that can be used in IPPs to improve the transliterating skills of students. The task of transliterating should be taught to students only after they have taken at least one interpreting skills class and have been taught the interpreting models and the process of interpreting.

The second goal of this book is to improve the transliterating skills of interpreters who have graduated from IPPs. This book will provide interpreters with a better understanding of the components of transliterating. Those interpreters will then be better able to pass the test and receive the Certificate for Transliteration from the National Registry of Interpreters for the Deaf.

The task of transliterating is just beginning to be defined in our profession. This book is an accumulation of my work, my observations as a transliterator, and other research in the field. The study of transliterating is an evolving process that can only be enhanced by the contributions of others

■■ INTRODUCTION

This book examines how transliterators use an English-based sign language when working with Deaf adults. This book is not intended to be used in any way to teach Deaf children English.

TARGET AUDIENCE

In Interpreting Preparation Programs (IPPs), the main focus of instruction and resources is on the task of interpreting. Few, if any, texts exist that cover the task of transliterating. This book was written to fill that need. It provides a comprehensive overview of the task of transliterating, and its primary goal is to serve as a standardized curriculum for students currently enrolled in IPPs who have taken at least one semester of interpreting skills.

The second goal of this book is to help interpreters who have graduated from IPPs but want to improve their transliterating skills. This book will provide working interpreters with a clearer understanding of the components that make up the task of transliterating.

HOW TO USE THIS BOOK

The book looks at four general areas. Chapters 1 through 3 look at why we transliterate, how transliterating and interpreting are similar and different, and how to make modifications to the English language during transliterating.

Chapter 4 looks at mouth movements and how transliterating differs from oral transliteration and interpretation.

Chapters 5 through 10 explore the nuts and bolts of going from a linear/auditory language to a spatial/visual language.

Chapter 11 discusses ways to evaluate your skills, as well as strategies for improving your transliterating.

There are exercises at the end of each chapter. In a classroom setting, these exercises can be done in small groups and then discussed as a class. Working interpreters are encouraged to work with another interpreter, or perhaps a mentor, for these exercises.

CHAPTER 1

Transliterating: The Beginning

Irene Interpreter is getting ready to begin her workday. Before she leaves the house, she checks her calendar to refresh her memory of what is scheduled for the day. 7:30 a.m. Breakfast meeting for ADA Task Force. Attending: Deaf director of the local agency for Deaf services. Strong ASL user. 10:00 a.m. Nutrition class. The consumer is a middle-aged Deaf woman, married to a Deaf man. Both attended the same school for the Deaf in the Midwest. The Deaf woman is in the early stages of diabetes and needs to learn how to change her eating habits. 1-5 p.m. Workshop on Teaching Literacy to K-3rd Graders, Part 2. Attending is a Deaf man currently teaching 2nd and 3rd graders in a contained Deaf program. When Irene interpreted Part 1 of this workshop, the consumer asked her and her partner to make sure to show him the English terms used to explain the program. Ok, a normal day. Irene closes her book and heads out the door.

As sign language interpreters, we are called on to either interpret or transliterate during the course of our work. Many interpreters are clear on what is needed when interpreting, but transliterating? This book is written as a beginning course on the task of transliteration.

The task of interpretation is taught in Interpreter Preparation Programs (IPPs) across the United States, yet there are differing opinions as to whether transliteration should even be taught in these programs, as transliterating is not a language (Kelly, 1999). There is also the question of whether or not transliteration is a form of oppression, because it is not the language of the Deaf. This feeling of oppression has been felt by the Deaf community as sign systems have been implemented by outsiders to "help the Deaf" learn English. But my experience as an interpreter has been that Deaf consumers, fluent in ASL, often ask, "Show me the English." As an interpreter, I had to learn what these Deaf consumers meant.

Through trial and error, research, and consumer feedback, I taught myself the task of transliterating, along with the ability to interpret. As interpreters we need both skills in order to provide Deaf consumers with whatever they request, and provide them with the best we have to offer. The purpose of this book, then, is not to downplay interpreting, but rather to elevate transliterating to an equal level of skill and respect in the field of interpreting.

In the course of their work, interpreters will encounter Deaf individuals who are culturally Deaf and choose to be bicultural. These Deaf individuals move easily between English and ASL. There are also Deaf individuals who choose transliterating rather than interpreting because of their own personal preference. These individuals may be late-deafened adults, Deaf adults educated in mainstream programs, or Deaf individuals who choose, in certain situations, to depend more on the English language than on American Sign Language (ASL) for their information. These individuals are still using a sign language, but it is based more on English than ASL.

Whether a sign language interpreter interprets or transliterates, the decision should not be based on the interpreter's wants, but rather on the consumer's preference. A consumer may always prefer transliterating over interpreting, or perhaps for a particular setting the consumer may choose transliteration. A history class in a community college may be better suited to interpreting for the consumer; but in an English grammar class, the consumer may prefer transliteration. Deaf consumers fluent in ASL will sometimes ask for transliterating during workshops, business meetings, or college courses because they want the specific English vocabulary. Viera (2000) performed a survey of Deaf consumers that use transliteration and found one typical answer as to why consumers sometimes choose transliteration:

> "I want to learn the language my (hearing) peers are using so I can respond in-kind. If I reply using their language, my peers know that I understand them."

When interpreters go to an assignment and transliterate, they cannot assume that as facilitators of communication they can simply "put English on their hands" and make sense to Deaf consumers. Unless the task of transliterating is truly understood, and the transliterator is making a conscious decision about the output of the transliteration, the message may not be clear. With an English-based sign language, it is critical to understand which components are significant. This is important because sign language, whether ASL or English-based, depends on how the language is perceived in a visual, not auditory, mode.

Throughout this book, the task of transliterating will be broken down into its different components. But overall, the task of transliterating is defined as delivering the signed message based on English grammatical order; basing sign choices on ASL usage, not English gloss; maintaining the meaning and intent of the original English; and understanding that the meaning of the message is more important than the form.

THE BEGINNING OF TRANSLITERATION

In 1965, the U.S. Department of Health, Education, and Welfare published the first book on interpreting, *Interpreting for Deaf People* (Quigley & Youngs, 1965). In this book, the term "translating" is used instead of "transliterating." The idea presented by the authors is that translating is what sign language interpreters do for highly literate Deaf persons who prefer to have their thoughts and those of the English speakers expressed verbatim. Yet even in 1965, it was recognized that when interpreters could not go literally from English to English-based sign language and still make sense, the interpreter would need to revert to ASL to get the point across.

In *Interpreting for Deaf People*, Quigley and Youngs explained that if an interpreter were at an assignment working as a "translator" and an English idiom came up, the translator might need to move into an interpreting process to clarify what was being said. This shows that from the very beginning of interpreter training, *meaning* was the utmost priority in an interpreter's job, whether the task was interpreting or translating.

In 1974, Robert Ingram (1974) proposed that *transliteration* would be a better term than *translation* to describe the process of going from a spoken modality to a signed modality while staying within the same language. The term *transliteration* was adopted by the field of sign language interpreting based on Ingram's writings (Siple, 1997). In 1979, the RID Code of Ethics, which originally contained only the term *interpreter*, was revised to include this new term. Now each tenet uses the more appropriate wording, "Interpreters/transliterators..." (Caccamise, et al., 1980).

In October 1983, at Madonna College, grant monies brought seven experienced interpreters together for the purpose of doing a task analysis of sign language interpretation and transliteration (McIntire, 1986). This group devised a rough draft and sent it to 20 people in the field for feedback. The revised draft then came to the 1984 Conference of Interpreter Trainers (CIT) in Asilomar, CA.

The result of this work was published in *New Dimensions in Interpreter Education: Task Analysis. Theory and Application* (McIntire, 1986). The writers concluded that transliterators needed to be aware that they will be "faced with contradictory or inconsistent linguistic, cultural, and/or effective input" (p. 94). It was also noted that "transliteration often requires certain modifications or adjustments to the incoming message" (p. 96). Transliterators were forewarned they would have to do a tremendous amount of work in order to make sense of the transliterated message.

Since 1972, the Registry of Interpreters for the Deaf (RID) has been evaluating interpreters by performance testing. In 1972, at RID's second convention, "it was decided to conduct a national evaluation of interpreters" (Zola, 1980, p. 6). From 1972 until 1989, successful candidates received a Comprehensive Skills Certificate (CSC). This certificate stated that holders of this certificate were capable of both interpreting and transliterating. Interpreters who did not attain adequate scores to warrant full certification were awarded an Interpretation Certificate (IC), a Transliteration Certificate (CT), or both.

In 1989 the concept of taking one test for both interpreting and transliterating changed (Humphrey & Alcorn, 1995). The membership of RID recognized that transliterating and interpreting were completely different tasks and warranted separate certificates and separate tests. Instead of one all-encompassing test, RID divided the performance test into three components. One component was a 150-question multiple-choice Generalist Written Test that covered general socio-cultural systems, language and language use, socio-political context interpreting, and interpreting and professional issues. After passing the Generalist Written Test, the candidate could then move on to the component that assessed interpreting skills or the component that assessed transliterating skills (RID, 1993).

In 1989, Elizabeth A. Winston wrote an article called, "Transliteration: What's the Message?" In this article, Winston looked at the task of transliterating in detail. She examined the complex combination of features in ASL and English, as well as the conscious strategies utilized during the task of transliterating. From 1990 to 1995, the average pass rate for the Certificate of Transliteration was 39% (Personal correspondence with RID, 1999). It seemed candidates taking the transliterating performance test lacked a clear understanding of what was expected of them, and RID was asked to state what their goals were for this examination (Matthews, 1995).

From Winston's article, RID drew up a concise half-page definition of 10 components that made up the task of transliterating. This definition of transliteration was published in RID's monthly publication, *VIEWS* (Winston, 1996). Between 1996, when the definition of the task of transliterating became available, and 1998, the pass rate was just over 68%.

SIGN SYSTEMS

Before Winston's article in 1989, practitioners and educators had tried to come up with a concise definition of transliteration. In Nancy Frishberg's text *Interpreting: An Introduction* (1990), she states that transliterating refers "to the process of changing an English text into Manually Coded English" (p. 19). This definition is correct but not helpful in breaking down and understanding the components that make up the task of transliterating.

There are English-based signing systems, referred to as Manually Coded English, which were developed to change English into a manual/visual mode (Neuman, 1981). These manual codes are not languages, but rather attempts to reflect the structure and vocabulary of English (Baker-Shenk, 1987). These sign codes include the Rochester method, Seeing Essential English (SEE I), Signing Exact English (SEE II), Signed English (SE), and Conceptually Accurate Signed English (CASE) (Humphrey & Alcorn, 1995). Below is a brief description of each sign code.

Seeing Essential English (SEE I)

SEE I is a coded sign system that came out of an experiment in 1966 to teach English to mentally retarded Deaf adults in Michigan (Lane et al., 1996). This work, led by David Anthony, a Deaf man of Deaf parents and an instructor at the Michigan School for the Deaf, was continued by others in California, who sought to apply it in the education of Deaf children and adults.

SEE I is based on the idea that there is a separate sign or movement for each English morpheme. A morpheme is the smallest meaningful unit of a word. Signs in SEE I are based not on meaning, but on the spelling of English syllables. No consideration is given to the conceptual accuracy of the sign used. Signs for prefixes and suffixes such as *ing* and *ment* have been invented, along with movements that indicate English verb conjugations.

Signing Exact English (SEE II)

SEE II is the result of a group of Deaf individuals, parents of Deaf children, children of Deaf parents, teachers of the Deaf, interpreters, and program administrators who met in southern California in January of 1969 "to discuss appropriate, effective ways to represent English in a gestural mode" (Gustason & Zawolkow, 1993). This is the most widely used Manually Coded English system in the United States today (Lane et al, 1996).

In SEE II, words are considered to belong to one of three groups: basic words, complex words, and compound words (Zawolkow, 1978). A basic word forms a complete word, and nothing can be taken away from it and still have it retain meaning; for example, *boy* or *hit*. This system follows the principle that "a sign should be translatable to only one English equivalent" (Gustason et al., 1980). "SEE has followed a 'one-word, one-sign' criterion in sign-selection for most words, despite their multiple meanings in English" (Gustason & Zawolkow, 1993). But understanding that the sign and the meaning may be unrelated, the authors state that "the basic sign can be altered slightly to express each separate meaning more clearly." The 1993 book *Signing Exact English* states that for basic words, "the three-point criteria of sound, spelling, and meaning is utilized. If any two of these three factors are the same, the same sign is used." For example, the word *run* is used in each of the following sentences:

I will *run* in the 800-meter race.

Sue will *run* for class president.

My nose will *run* if I catch a cold.

In SEE II, *run* would be signed the same way for each sentence, even though it would be signed differently in ASL. The outcome of this three-point criteria gave sound and form precedence over the meaning of the word (Moores, 1977).

Complex words are basic words with the addition of an affix, such as *s*, or an inflection, such as *ing*, to show continuation. The signer takes a basic word, such as *boy* or *hit* and adds an *s* or *ing* to sign BOYS or HITTING. The three-point criterion still applies.

Compound words are two or more basic words put together. If the meanings of the basic words separately are consistent with the compound meaning, then they are signed as two separate signs. Thus, the word *underline* is signed UNDER + LINE. But if the meanings of the two basic words are inconsistent with the meaning of the compound word, then the compound word is signed differently. For example, the English word *understand* has no relation to the meanings of the English words *under* and *stand*; therefore, a different sign is used for UNDERSTAND.

Signed English (SE)

SE is a system of signs that combines English grammatical order with signs from ASL along with invented initialized signs. This system was developed to get rid of the "two out of three" rule of SEE II and, instead, create "sign markers" that are added to signs to more accurately represent English. Structurally, it is the least complicated of the manual English systems (Bornstein, 1987). In addition, the authors of SE have the philosophy that if there is no ASL sign for an English word already in place, instead of fingerspelling the word, a sign should be made up. In the book *Comprehensive Signed English Dictionary* (Bornstein, Hamilton, & Saulnier, 1983), over one-third of the 3,000 entries are signs made up by the authors (Stedt & Moores, 1990).

Conceptually Accurate Signed English (CASE)

CASE is a term that refers to the use of signs based on the meaning of the idea being conveyed rather than the English word that is being used (Humphrey & Alcorn, 1995). In this system, meaning has primary importance over sound and spelling of the word. Signs are produced following English sentence structure, and these signs are often used with spoken or mouthed English, but retain ASL features, such as use of space and facial markers.

In the CASE signing system, the word RUN would use a different sign in the three samples that were used for SEE II.

SO WHAT'S A TRANSLITERATOR TO DO?

With so many sign systems and conflicting ideas of how to sign when you want to convey English rather than ASL, three questions arise:

> Which variety of signed systems should be used by the transliterator?

> What can be expected from the transliterator by any given consumer?

> What components of ASL and English are brought into the task of transliterating?

CASE is the sign system that the transliterator will be most dependent on when transliterating. The 1984 Conference of Interpreter Trainers put the idea of transliterating to discussion and tried to discover how transliterators added clarity and meaning to the inadequate form of signed English. These strategies turned out to be various borrowings from ASL, which will be discussed later in this book.

The terminology of transliterating has also changed throughout the years. "Pidgin Sign English" was the term once used to described what happened when English and ASL users came together to communicate (Cassell & McCaffrey, 1995). It was neither ASL nor English, but a blended form of both. This blending of ASL and English is now being either referred to as "contact language" or "Anglicized sign language" (Bragg, 1989).

THE CONSUMERS OF TRANSLITERATION

As we continue to work on expanding our knowledge of ASL, we must recognize that not all Deaf people are fluent in ASL or choose to always use ASL. Kannapell (1982) observed six variations in communication styles that she believes exists within the Deaf community:

ASL monolinguals. Deaf people who express themselves only in ASL. They have no skills in English.

ASL-dominant bilinguals. Deaf people who are more comfortable expressing themselves in ASL than in English.

Balanced bilinguals. Deaf people who are comfortable expressing themselves in ASL and English and are able to understand both equally well.

English-dominant bilinguals. Deaf people who are more comfortable expressing themselves in English than in ASL.

English monolinguals. Deaf people who are comfortable expressing themselves only in English, either by oral or signed English. They have no skills in ASL.

Semi-lingual. Deaf people who have some skills in both English and ASL, but have not mastered either language.

The preference to use an English-based sign language is based on the needs of the client and/or the context of the setting (Kannapell, 1989). This code switching, common to many bilingual communities, is referred to as "diglossia" (Woodward, 1987). There is considerable diversity within the population that uses transliterators (Viera, 2000). Consumers may be male or female. They may have varying degrees of hearing loss. They may have been born Deaf or become Deaf later in life. They may be high school graduates or hold degrees and may work in academic settings or business settings. They may have learned sign language either as adults or as children.

In 1995, the Research and Training Center on Mental Health for Persons Who Are Hard-of-Hearing or Late-Deafened stated that there were an estimated 800,000 to 1,500,000 people who were late-deafened, while 20,000,000 people were classified as hard-of-hearing, and 600,000 to 1,000,000 people were prelingually/culturally Deaf.

Another consumer of transliterating may be a Deaf adult proficient in ASL who wants the English vocabulary that is being presented verbatim. This person may feel that in a particular situation, such as a classroom setting, the English is as critical as the information itself (Woodward, 1987). In these situations, the consumer may ask the interpreter to stay closer to the English grammar, rather than interpreting into ASL.

With the passage of Section 504 of the Rehabilitation Act of 1973, Public Law 93-112, and the Americans with Disabilities Act of 1991, there has been more access to communication, employment, government services, and telecommunications for Deaf people than ever before (Warner, 1987). These consumers want both interpreting and transliterating. The needs of individuals who request transliteration can be better served by sign language interpreters who understand how to transliterate.

SUMMARY

While Interpreting Preparation Programs, books, and videos can help a person to become an interpreter, very few materials are available to help with becoming a transliterator. Although consumers often ask interpreters to transliterate, many interpreters are unclear about what constitutes the process of transliteration. This lack of understanding causes a lack of standardized expectation on the part of the provider and the consumer.

The idea of transliterating has been around since 1964, with the first published book *Interpreting for Deaf People* (Quigley & Youngs, 1965). At that time, transliterating was referred to as "translating." The idea of translating was to take the words expressed by the English speaker and translate them verbatim for highly literate Deaf persons. If an English idiom came up, or when a concept was unclear during translation, however, the translator would be expected to switch to interpreting.

The term *transliterator* was established in 1979, and RID revised their original Code of Ethics to include this term. Each of the eight tenets of the Code of Ethics now starts with the words "Interpreters/transliterators...." The role of the transliterator was defined by the Conference of Interpreter Trainers when they performed a task analysis of sign language interpretation and transliteration in 1984, at their conference in Asilomar, CA. In 1989, RID developed and offered, for the first time, separate tests for the tasks of interpreting and transliterating.

With all the sign systems that have been created, there is sometimes confusion as to what is expected of the transliterator. Which variety of signed systems should be used? What is expected of the transliterator? Is the English word more important than the meaning? There is also a vast array of language abilities among Deaf consumers. The transliterator cannot expect all consumers to have the same needs or requirements.

ACTIVITIES

Activity 1-1

Discussion and group work on usage of English-based signing and ASL.

Step 1. Form into small groups of 4-6 people.

Step 2. Discuss the following questions:

1. Have you seen a Deaf person use English-based signing?

2. If the person using English-based signing knows ASL, why do you think they chose not to use ASL in that particular situation?

3. When would you expect to see a Deaf person use English-based signing?

4. Is English-based signing considered a language, with grammatical syntax and cultural affiliation, like ASL?

5. How is transliterating different from signing SEE I, SEE II, and Signed English?

Step 3. Come back together and discuss your answers as a group.

Activity 1-2

Discussion and group work regarding differences and similarities of English-based signing and ASL.

Step 1. Watch a videotape supplied by your instructor of Deaf individuals using English-based signing.

Step 2. While watching the tape, write down the differences between English-based sign language and ASL. Write down the similarities of English-based sign language and ASL.

Step 3. While watching the tape, write down the differences between English-based sign language and English. Write down the similarities between English-based sign language and English.

Step 4. Discuss how Deaf people use an English-based signing system. What might a transliterator do that is similar or different?

■■ CHAPTER 2

Interpretation vs. Transliteration

THE BUILDING BLOCKS OF TRANSLITERATION

When interpreters perform the task of transliterating, they do so to meet the needs of the consumer. Whatever reason the Deaf consumer might have for choosing transliterating rather than interpreting, the goal of the interpreter should be to provide the best transliterating possible.

Before interpreters can transliterate, however, they need to have mastered the building blocks that make up the task of transliterating. These basic skills of transliterating do not occur as separate items, but rather overlap and are continuously learned over time. The building blocks, or prerequisites, of transliterating are listed below:

- A good command of the English language

- A good command of ASL

- Appropriate understanding and usage of grammar and vocabulary of both languages

A Good Command of the English Language

A transliterator must truly understand the nuances, slang, meanings, and purposes of words in English. This is no small task. The average English dictionary found in any home contains over 155,000 words (American Heritage Dictionary, 1999). These 155,000 words do not include the other half-million technical and scientific terms that are not catalogued (McCrum et al., 1987). Any transliterator who plans to work in a technical field should be familiar with all the terms used in that particular discipline.

A Good Command of American Sign Language

ASL does not have as many signs as the English language has words, but that does not mean that ASL is inferior or less of a language than English is. An individual who truly understands ASL will know that it is not only the sign itself that carries meaning, but also the use of space, the temporal aspect of the sign, and the non-manual markers that add to the conveyance of the message. Deaf adults, whether asking for interpreting or transliterating, still need cues that are natural to a visual language. When a Deaf adult asks for transliterating, the signed message is clearer when features of ASL that enhance the English-based signed message are also used.

There is the idea that ASL is a "conceptual" language. But all languages are conceptual. The real point is not whether a sign is conceptual or not, but how a particular language chooses to package concepts. In ASL, more information can be packed into a typical ASL sign than into a typical English word (Wilcox & Wilcox, 1991).

Appropriate Use of Grammar and Vocabulary

The appropriate use of grammar and vocabulary is necessary for both ASL and English. Transliterators need to understand how ASL uses characterization, subject-object agreement, and verb inflections. It is also critical to understand how English uses words to make a point, how tone and inflection change the meaning of a sentence, and how the use of voice works.

Understanding the grammars of ASL and English is an asset to a transliterator. It is also important to understand conversation regulators in English and ASL, what classifiers represent in English, how pronominalizations are used in ASL, and the temporal and distributional aspects of ASL. These areas are as critical to transliterators as they are to interpreters.

INTERPRETATION VS. TRANSLITERATION

Spoken language interpreters use the term *translation* to refer to "changing messages from one language into another"(Frishberg, 1990, p. 18). In the field of sign language interpretation, we do not translate into a written form; however, the profession did use the term "translate" in 1965 when referring to English-like signing done by an interpreter (Quigley & Youngs, 1965). In 1974 the term *transliteration* replaced *translating* to refer to "the process of changing an English text into Manually Coded English (or vice versa)" (Frishberg, 1990, p.19).

In systems using Manually Coded English, the features and form of English often influence the sign choice rather than being guided by the meaning of the sign. In contrast, transliterating gives more weight to ASL features and the meaning of the message when deciding which sign to use.

If the transliterator lacks training or lacks a clear idea of the components that make up the task of transliterating, then the target message may not be an accurate representation of what the speaker is trying to convey. The first step in performing the task of transliterating is to understand the similarities and differences between the tasks of interpreting and transliterating.

Similarities between Interpreting and Transliterating

When interpreters perform the task of transliterating, they must recognize that there are similarities between interpreting and transliterating.

- Clarity in the production of signing and fingerspelling

- Use of non-manual behaviors

- Use of space

- Sign vocabulary choice and utilization

- Message conveyance

Clarity in the Production of Signing and Fingerspelling

The signs used in transliterating are the same signs used in interpreting and should be produced by following the same parameters (Klima & Bellugi, 1979):

Hand configuration. The general element that includes the hand shape (/A/, /B/, /C/, etc.).

Movement. The complex element describing a sign's change of hand-shape (the hand's internal movement) or orientation (wrist movement), and/or the point of articulation (directional, circular, interaction movement).

Palm orientation. The orientation of the palm in relationship to the body and the hand arrangement (the number of hands involved).

Location. The location in the signing space where a sign is produced and the part of the hand that contacts the other hand or body.

Any fingerspelling that is done by the transliterator should be smooth and fluent. "Fluency refers to the ability of the speller to generate automatically individual handshapes and time them in a smooth sequence" (Akamatsu & Stewart, 1989, p. 370). Transliterators follow the same rules of fingerspelling as interpreters.

Use of Non-Manual Behaviors

Whether interpreting or transliterating, what is being produced on the hands is still being produced in a visual, rather than auditory, mode. As sign language is a visual form of communication, the grammatical markers of ASL are conveyed on the face. Appropriate facial markers need to also occur in transliterating. These facial markers include, but are not limited to, question markers, conditional sentence markers, and topic markers. Facial markers also add stress and intonation to a visual language. Without these markers, the transliteration becomes monotone.

Use of Space

Spoken English is an oral language that is produced sequentially (Humphrey & Alcorn, 1995). ASL is a spatial language based on visual perception and conveyance (Baker & Cokely, 1980). Because of these differences, the transliterator needs to be aware of the implications of going from spoken English to an English-based sign language. The transliterator retains the word order of English but uses the ASL feature of space. To do this, the transliterator must be clear in the placement of persons, places, and objects, just as an interpreter would. Use of space involves body shifts and use of pronouns and modulating verbs.

Sign Vocabulary and Utilization

Transliterators do not have to learn new signs to perform the task of transliterating. But transliterators do need to understand that there are differences in the way signs are presented grammatically. While interpreting, grammatical choices are made when interpreting from English to ASL. Within transliterating there are grammatical issues unique to the task that are not found in the task of interpreting. These grammatical issues will be discussed in Chapters 7, 8, and 9.

The range of vocabulary, the variety of signs, the use of signs based on ASL usage, and an understanding of register are as critical to a transliterator as they are to an interpreter.

Message Conveyance

When all is said and done, the two questions that must be asked are "Did the transliteration make any sense?" and "Did the consumer understand the message?" The task of transliterating is not successful if you get all the signs right but the message is unclear.

Differences between Interpreting and Transliterating

When interpreters transliterate, they must recognize that there are differences between transliterating and interpreting.

- Processing time
- Deletion of words and phrases
- Mouth movements

Processing Time

Processing, in its simplest form, refers to the input of information, the analysis of information, and the output of information. There are four levels of processing: lexical, phrasal, sentential, and textual (Colonomos, 1989). These levels move from a word-by-word level to a whole-text level.

Lexical. This level focuses on the text word-by-word. Each word is looked at individually without regard to how the other words affect that word.

Phrasal. This level occurs when two or more words together in a phrase have a different meaning than the individual words. For example, *I ran into Jim* contains the phrase *ran into*. These two words together do not mean that I physically ran into Jim, but that I "met" Jim or "saw" Jim. Another example is *the baby fell asleep*. The baby does not actually "fall" here. Rather, the word *fall* goes with *asleep* to make one concept.

Sentential. This level deals with concepts produced in full sentences. The basic sentence contains a subject, a verb, and an object. *The boy threw the ball* is a basic sentence. *The boy* is the subject, *threw* is the verb, and *the ball* is the object. Adjectives and adverbs can be added to lengthen the sentence.

Textual. This level looks at the whole text used to convey an idea. Information given out earlier in a text may impact how a word is used later.

Because the transliterator is more concerned with English word order than an interpreter, the length of processing and the amount of time the transliterator waits between receiving a message and the output are often shorter. This occurs because transliterators are trying to retain the original word order, retain the meaning of the source message, and produce an English-based sign language. For these reasons, most of the transliterator's work is performed at the lexical and phrasal levels.

There are problems that occur when working at the lexical and phrasal levels. Without enough processing time, the wrong meaning might be given to a word that has multiple meanings. When we look at passive sentences in Chapter 10, we see that transliterators must go beyond the phrasal level and process at the sentential level to enhance clarity. Transliterators must also be cognizant of what is happening at the textual level to ensure that what they are transliterating is accurate. Knowing the context helps transliterators make appropriate sign choices.

Deletion of Words and Phrases

English speakers talk at the rate of about 180 words per minute (Isenhath, 1990). An interpreter can transmit this information into ASL at approximately the same rate (Klima & Bellugi, 1979). But it is impossible for a transliterator to produce every word or phrase presented in English. Even if a transliterator were able to keep up with the speed of the message, the signs would be produced so quickly that clarity would be lost, use of space would be compromised, and facial markers would become sloppy.

The focus of transliterating is to convey the meaning of the speaker by using an

English-based sign language, so the transliterator needs to be pragmatic. If there is a lot of redundancy in the original English message that does not add to the overall meaning, the redundancy can be eliminated to make the transliterated message clearer. Some words can be incorporated into signs by modulation of the verb while still ensuring that the information is conveyed and the English word order is maintained. Also, articles are deleted during the task of transliterating.

Mouth Movements

When interpreting, the mouth patterns of the interpreter reflect appropriate adult ASL usage. In transliteration, cohesive English sentences are visibly presented on the lips, either the exact words from the original text or English paraphrasing of the original text. During transliterating, the non-audible English that is mouthed should not be exaggerated, nor should there be sub-verbal noise or mumbling.

TRANSLITERATING TODAY

Transliterating is more than simply recoding spoken English into English-based sign language. The task of transliterating includes a complex combination of features from ASL and English that are accomplished by conscious strategies employed by the transliterator (Winston, 1989). These strategies are considered conscious because the choices are planned by the transliterator rather than being randomly or erroneously produced.

Features from English

Transliterators provide a visual target form that not only resembles spoken English structure and syntax, but is also comprehensible to someone who is not using an auditory language. For this reason, it is appropriate to use forms that are specific to visual languages to achieve clarity and meaning in the signed message. At the same time, it is appropriate to include the visual feature of English. This feature is the mouthing of the English words.

In transliteration, the following features from English are included:

- English word order

- English words are mouthed

Features from American Sign Language

When transliterators go from spoken English to an English-based sign language using signs based on ASL usage, they do not simply sign in English word order in a linear fashion. Transliterators need to use the visual features of ASL to clarify and enhance the English-based sign language message. The use of visual features from ASL is a logical result when trying to use a visual form of a spoken language.

ASL has features that must be incorporated into a transliterated text, even when not following the grammatical features of ASL. Transliterators will include the following features from ASL:

1. Lexical choice
2. Head and body shifting for marking phrases and clauses
3. Use of location
4. Verb modulation (inflections)
5. Facial markers, non-manual markers

This combination of features from English and ASL, rather than confusing the consumer, provides enough detail to produce a clearer message. These features reflect conscious strategies used by transliterators during analysis and production of the target message. The goals of the transliterator are to:

1. Deliver the message based on English grammatical order
2. Remember that meaning and understanding come before form
3. Use signs based on ASL usage and not on English gloss
4. Maintain the meaning and intent of the original English

SUMMARY

To do the job well, transliterators must have a good command of the English language as well as a good command of ASL. They must also understand how both languages present information through grammatical choices. There are some similarities between the tasks of interpreting and transliterating:

- The need to be clear when signing and fingerspelling

- Use of non-manual behaviors

- Use of space

- Sign choices

- The need to make sure the message is conveyed in such a way that the consumer understands

There are also differences between the tasks of interpreting and transliterating:

- The amount of information that is processed at one time

- The deletion of words and phrases

- The use of mouth movements

In transliterating, there is a conscious strategy used by the transliterator to produce the message in an English-based sign language while maintaining meaning. To accomplish this, the transliterator is aware of features borrowed from English, such as English word order and mouthing of the English words. Transliterators also need to be aware of features borrowed from ASL, such as lexical choices, head and body shifting, use of location, verb modulation, and use of facial and non-manual markers.

The transliterator works to produce a message that is understood by the consumer. The transliterator keeps four goals in mind;

1. Deliver the message based on English grammatical order

2. Remember that meaning and understanding come before form

3. Use signs based on ASL usage, not on English gloss

4. Maintain the meaning and intent of the original English

ACTIVITIES

Activity 2-1

Discussion and group work.

The model of interpreting below (Roy, 1980) states that an interpreter must:

1. Receive the auditory/visual message

2. Already possess fluency in two languages

3. Be conversant with the subject matter and refer to pre-existing knowledge

4. Comprehend the message (source language)

5. Analyze the message thoroughly: identify interrelationships within the message, and recognize other meaningful elements, such as gestures, facial expression, style of delivery, changes in volume, intensity, body language, etc.

6. Discard wording, but at the same time,

7. Retain non-verbal thought through a process of visualization, seek equivalents

8. Recreate the message in the target language

9. Produce an oral/gestural-motoric message

Step 1. As a class, discuss the above model of interpreting.

Step 2. Divide into groups of 4-5 people and discuss how the process of transliterating is similar to the process of interpreting. Write down these similarities.

Step 3. In your groups, discuss how the process of transliterating is different from the process of interpreting. Write down these differences.

Step 4. Discuss whether you feel the task of interpreting or the task of transliterating is harder to master. Defend your reasons.

Step 5. Come together as a class and compare your answers.

Activity 2-2

Establishing a baseline.

To measure the improvement in your transliterating skills, a baseline needs to be established. Students should record a 10-minute sample of their transliterating skills. The material used can be chosen by the students or provided by the instructor.

Do not evaluate or observe this tape now. Keep the tape in a safe place until the end of the semester. Near the end of the semester, using the same spoken-English material as before, transliterate the material. At that time, you will review both tapes.

Activity 2-3

Process levels.

Take the following text and break it into either lexical or phrasal levels based on what you think is critical for meaning. If the meaning of a word changes by the words preceding it or after it, or the placement of a sign is affected, those words should be included together in a level. Give a rationale for your decisions.

> **Example:**
>
> On Michigan's Isle Royale/scientists/have a rare chance/to study/a simple food chain at work.
>
> > **On Michigan's Isle Royal** *(because the name of the island is one phrase)* **scientists** *(the word scientist would not change because of where they are)* **have a rare chance** *(rare is used to define chance)* **to study** *(the word study can stand alone)* **a simple food chain at work** *(the word work is related to the food chain, and the sign choice would change).*

At the bottom of this food chain, there are several kinds of plants. They store energy from sunlight as food. Herbivores (plant eaters) are in the middle of the chain. They get their energy by eating the plants. These herbivores include 1,000 to 2,000 moose, which eat most of the plants.

At the top of the food chain are carnivores, which get their energy by eating meat. On Isle Royale, the only carnivores are 25 to 50 wolves. Their diet is mainly moose.

In most wild habitats, the food chains are hard to understand. Usually, several chains are tangled together. In these food "webs," two or three kinds of meat eaters may live off several types of plant eaters, which may feed on many kinds of plants. Compared to food webs, Isle Royale is a simple laboratory set up by nature.

For 25 years, Dr. Rolf Peterson has been studying this habitat. He is a wildlife ecologist at Michigan Tech University. By flying over the island in an airplane, he and other scientists watch and count the animals. Scientists hope to understand the complex systems of food chains called food webs. But first, they have to learn more about simple food chains, partly by studying the wolves, moose, and trees that live on Isle Royale.

(Boyles, 1996, p. 8)

CHAPTER 3

Modifications to the English Structure

LITERAL VS. IDIOMATIC TRANSLITERATION

So far, we have concentrated on how interpreters transliterate from English to an English-based sign language. However, there are certain considerations a transliterator must be aware of when transliterating from an English-based sign language into English. When observing what is signed and interpreting it into English, the primary goal is always to make sense of the message. In other words, meaning is more important than form. For this reason, a transliterator may have to make adjustments to the way the English-based sign language message is presented in the source language so that it makes sense in the target language, English.

Idiomatic Phrasing in English

All languages have idioms. Idioms are speech forms that are peculiar to a given language, or a specialized vocabulary used by a group of people (Morris, 1980). An aphorism, or saying, is one type of idiom that is used to pass down a truth or opinion. These are usually full sentences, such as *That is water under the bridge* or *Don't count your chickens before they hatch*. Idioms include phrases such as *bread and butter* or *ladies and gentlemen*. These are often referred to as "figures of speech." Idiomatic phrasing is the unique way a given language is presented.

Deaf consumers using an English-based signing system will sometimes sign a phrase that, if voiced verbatim, would not be the most natural or idiomatic way to present the phrase in English. For example, during a Christmas play, a Deaf woman onstage was telling the audience the Christmas story about Mary and Joseph going to Bethlehem. In the middle of the story, the Deaf woman signed NO ROOM IN HOTEL. The word used by people familiar with the story is *inn*, as in "There was no room at the *inn*." Yet the interpreter said "There was no room in the hotel." The sentence made sense, but it sounded wrong.

In Mildred L. Larson's book *Meaning-Based Translation: A Guide to Cross-Language Equivalence* (1984), she discusses the idea of translators doing literal translations that attempt to follow the form of the source language. Larson suggests that instead of a literal translation, a better way would be to use an idiomatic translation. Idiomatic translations make every attempt to communicate the meaning of the source language in the natural form of the target language. An example is the term *Y2K compliant*. Most transliterators or interpreters would sign the concept

FOLLOW+Y+2+K, but when a Deaf person signs during a presentation FOLLOW+Y+2+K, the English coming from the transliterator's mouth should be *Y2K compliant*.

Idiomatic Phrasing in an English-Based Sign Language

When interpreting English idioms into ASL, interpreters look for the meaning and then interpret the meaning into the target language in the most appropriate way for it to be understood in ASL. This is not always the case for transliterators, as some Deaf consumers want to see the English signed verbatim. A few English idioms are *jump to it, fly into a rage,* and *fell for it.* The meaning of an idiom comes from the combination of the words, not the individual words themselves. A word-for-word transliteration of idioms may or may not make sense to consumers. But when working with a Deaf person that requests transliteration, one should assume that this person "is sufficiently acculturated or bicultural to negotiate successful communication and cultural interactions" (Viera, 2000, p. 96). The transliterator must work with the consumer to decide whether idiomatic phrases should be transliterated word-for-word or for meaning.

Sign choices based on English grammar alone are not sufficient when going from English into an English-based transliteration. The transliterator must recognize that certain forms in the source language must be changed for the target language in order to make sense. Otherwise, the transliterator could end up with something comparable to the instruction sheet found in a toy made in Taiwan, a plastic boomerang called a "Fly Back Disk." The instructions read as follows:

> The people who achieves the mark of 21 points shall win the first round at first. The one who wins the four rounds at first shall be considered as winner.

The meaning of these instructions is that the first person to earn 21 points wins that round. The first person to win four rounds wins the game. The instructions make sense, but they are not idiomatically presented into English. Perhaps the instructions were written this way because the translation was based on the grammatical structure used in Taiwan. This example clearly shows that meaning does not occur simply by stringing words together in English. Within the target language, you have to look for the most natural way of presenting that language.

There are idiomatic expressions in every language. In English, when you tell someone to sit down, the idiomatic phrase is *take a seat*. When someone experiences a *hot time*, they are not talking about the weather. *I hear you* means you understood what was said, not that you were auditorially able to hear. Transliterators need to be aware of what these idiomatic phrases truly mean.

CLARIFYING THE TRANSLITERATED MESSAGE

Interpreters change form constantly in grammar, syntax, and idiomatic phrasing. When interpreting from English to ASL, or ASL to English, sometimes meaning is lost, as words do not have the same meaning in the two languages. It is the same for transliterators. Transliterators, wanting to retain meaning, use different ways to add clarity to the message. Ways to clarify the transliterated message are through *additions, restructuring,* and *deletions.*

Additions

Siple (1996) did a study on the use of additions in sign language transliteration. She found that transliterators frequently added information to the signed message to make it more comprehensible to Deaf consumers. Siple's main findings "showed that the transliterated target messages produced by the interpreters frequently contained information not directly found in the source message" (p. 39). Different ways information was added to the transliterated message included *cohesion, clarification, modality adaptation, repetition,* and *reduplication.*

Cohesion. "Cohesion is an addition that serves as a link to different parts of a discourse" (Siple, 1996, p. 33). For a transliterator this means adding spatial referencing and use of space. The use of space to establish a referent (indexing) is a feature used in ASL but not in English. In English, a referent is referred to as a pronoun.

The term to denote pronouns in ASL is *pronominalization.* After a noun is produced, the transliterator points to a space to signify that this space will now be used to represent the noun — a person, place, or thing — or a location previously assigned to the noun, as in the example below:

> Susan decided that she wanted to go home.

The addition to this sentence is to index a place that would represent *home.* Later, the transliterator references *home* by simply pointing to the space assigned. Again, indexing is used after a noun has been established. If a referent is used without a noun, there is no clear meaning as to what the referent represents.

Clarification. Clarification is "an addition that serves to make the source message clear and free of ambiguity" (Siple, 1996, p. 33). Clarification can be used in two ways: either by stating the implied meaning of the text, or by linking a particular English lexical item with a particular sign.

With implied meaning, addition is used when the signs themselves do not have the same meaning in ASL as they do in English. In the phrase,

> When we bring young and old together

the meaning implied is that young people and old people will come together. The transliterator adds the sign PEOPLE to clarify the meaning.

Linking a particular English lexical item with a particular sign occurs when a sign represents an English word that is not normally glossed for that meaning.

> Each one of you will take turns to facilitate the meeting.

In this phrase, transliterators can use the sign CONTROL to represent the English word *facilitate*. The transliterator first fingerspells F-A-C-I-L-I-T-A-T-E, then signs CONTROL to show that this sign is representing this specific English word.

Addition also refers to the use of a conceptually accurate sign or signs either before or after a more literal equivalent.

> The test is a week from today.

Here, transliterators can add the sign TUESDAY, or whatever day is a week from today, to the phrase *a week from today* to clarify when the test will be given.

Another use of addition is the negative headshake. A negative headshake negates signs or phrases used by the transliterator. This non-manual form is used syntactically in ASL to mark negative clauses and is seen as an addition whether or not a negating sign is used.

> If you don't plan to go, tell me before Friday.

A headshake during the conditional clause *If you don't plan to go* is a strategy for clarification.

Modality adaptation. The way a language is presented is referred to as its modality. The modality used by English is auditory/vocal, and the modality used by ASL is visual/sign. A modality adaptation is "an addition that visually communicates an auditory aspect of the language" (Siple, 1996, p. 33).

English is not a language made up of just words, but rather a language that contains a nonverbal aspect. Part of the nonverbal aspect of language is presented in the volume, rate, and tone of the speaker's voice (Miller, 1972).

Volume refers to whether the speaker is saying the word quietly or loudly. Rate refers to the speed of delivery–whether the speaker is talking slowly, moderately, or quickly. Tone refers to the pitch of the speaker's voice, such as the ability to make the words "nice haircut" sound like either a compliment or an insult.

Because the nonverbal aspect of English is based on auditory cues, the transliterator must listen to how volume, rate, and tone affect the English word. Based on this nonverbal information, transliterators can add implied meaning by the use of non-manual markers. Look at the following English sentence:

> It was a wonderful experience.

If, in this sentence, there was a pause between *it* and *was*, the pausing would add meaning that would need to be shown by adding facial markers, such as crunching up the nose. Or perhaps the speaker became choked up with emotion and was trying not to cry. That tonal quality cannot be seen on the speaker's face, so transliterators add this information by showing that the speaker is emotional.

Facial expressions add clarity to the visual message. Facial expressions, along with the sign, show what meaning is trying to be conveyed. Facial expressions also show when a topic begins or ends. Transliterators include non-manual markers of ASL on their face to mark separation of clauses, topic shifts, and sentence markers. If appropriate markers are not used, then the transliterator is seen as having run-on sentences flowing into each other. Some facial non-manual markers that transliterators use are for conditional clauses, rhetorical questions, topic markers, and yes/no questions.

Repetition. Repetition is "an addition that provides emphasis by repeating a key word or phrase" (Siple, 1996, p. 33). Although English tends not to repeat the topic, transliterators can retain English word order with the addition of repetition.

Transliterators use repetition to give importance to the information. If the story in English is about dressing children in a multi-layer of clothes because it is cold outside, the transliterator signs COLD at the end of the sentence to emphasize that the weather was really cold. Repetition is a natural part of a visual language, as the topic is often given at the beginning and at the end of a sentence. For the transliterator, this repetition enhances the clarity of the message.

Reduplication. Reduplication is "an addition that involves the reforming of a sign for the purpose of pluralization" (Siple, 1996, p .34). The word *teachers* would need a reduplication in the AGENT sign to show more than one teacher.

According to the study done by Siple (1996), these last two categories–repetition and reduplication–were used by transliterators to make the message more comprehensible, but not to the same degree as the first three categories–cohesion, clarification, and modality adaptation.

Restructuring

Restructuring "refers to the replacement of one grammatical structure with another" (Winston, 1989, p. 161). Restructuring involves one multi-word phrase replacing another multi-word phrase. Restructuring can occur in combination with any or all of the other features found in addition. In English, one concept can be expressed in several different ways, with the same meaning taking on different forms.

Example 1:

1. My house has three bedrooms.

2. My three-bedroom house.

3. My house, which has three bedrooms.

Example 2:

1. One out of four college students.

2. 25% of college students

3. 25 out of 100 college students.

In both examples, all three phrases have the same meaning but use different forms of conveying that meaning. In example 1, phrase A would be the easiest to transliterate, while phrase C would use deletion of the word *which*. In example 2, phrase B is signed following the English word order. The other two phrases would have to be restructured.

The reason transliterating is difficult is that there is no correlation between the form (lexicon and grammar) and the meaning (semantics). The transliterator must always be conscious of the need to convey meaning over form and still stay within the confines of English word order.

Another way restructuring occurs is when the English sentence structure is a verb followed by the subject:

Sailing west, the boat continued on.

The verb *sailing* occurs before the subject, *boat*. In a visual language, the verb *sailing* is easier to identify when the noun *boat* is presented first, then switched to a classifier. By restructuring the sentence to *The boat, sailing west, continued on*, the transliterator still maintains an English sentence structure with no meaning lost, and the message becomes clearer in the English-based sign language.

These restructured discourse fragments are accompanied by mouthing the English words that correspond to the restructured form being presented in the transliterated message. The original sentence structure from the source message is no longer maintained on the lips (Winston, 1989). If a transliterator restructured the sentence *Sailing west, the boat continued on* while signing *The boat, sailing west, continued on* and maintained the original sentence on the lips, I think the consumer would go cross-eyed. It is a great parlor trick, but not conducive to understanding.

Restructuring also occurs when there are double negatives in the English sentence. In English when a negation is in front of a negative word, the meaning of the text becomes positive. In other words, in English, two negatives make a positive. The use of two negatives in ASL emphasizes the negative; the second negation does not negate the negative. When transliterators hear two negative English words, they restructure by either dropping both negatives or using signs/compound signs that make the sentence positive.

The area was *not unlike* her hometown.

Transliterators would restructure the sentence to *The area was* like *her hometown*. In a more complicated sentence, the meaning must be discovered and presented in a clear manner.

Without doing more research, we cannot be sure who our consumers are.

This sentence is interesting as it has a negative word but a positive meaning of action. Transliterators can change the form of the sentence to *We need more research to know who our consumers are*.

Deletions

It is not always possible to keep up with the entire English output in the transliterated message; therefore, omissions are needed. "Many parts of English words and phrases are not necessary to the overall meaning in context; they are redundant" (Winston, 1989, p. 160). By deleting the redundancies, the transliterator produces a clearer message form while at the same time retaining the meaning.

As stated, English is produced at about 180 words per minute (Isenhath, 1990). Although ASL can transmit information at approximately the same rate as English (Klima & Bellugi, 1979), it is impossible for a transliterator to try to keep up with 180 spoken words per minute. This is because "ASL takes roughly double the amount of time to produce a single ASL sign compared to the time required for the utterance of a single English word" (Humphrey & Alcorn, 1995). To keep up without losing the message, transliterators may have to delete words during their work.

One example of deletion is when the transliterator has two sentences or phrases that have the same meaning. The transliterator retains one and deletes the other, signing the meaning clearly. In the sentence,

> We have come here, to this place, to celebrate

the phrases *come here* and *to this place* mean the same thing, so the transliterator deletes one of the phrases.

If a single word can replace a phrase in a sentence and retain the same meaning, then the transliterator replaces the phrase with the word. In the phrase,

> We have decided at this point in time

the phrase *at this point in time* means the same as "now." The transliterator deletes the phrase *at this point in time* and replaces it with the sign NOW.

Tense is another example when omission is used. In English, each past tense verb is marked with a tense indicator, such as in the sentence below:

> Yesterday, I ate my food while I walked to the store.

ASL users mark tense at the beginning of a topic, as in the use of YESTERDAY to mark the past tense. The tense for *eat* and *walk* does not have to be marked again until the tense changes. Because of this grammatical marking "the use of the past tense marker on each verb is unnecessary from the standpoint of context-bound, referential-and-predicational effectiveness" (Winston, 1989, p. 160). Transliterators delete tense markers for individual signs when recoding the English message once the tense marker has been used. Other tense markers are *tomorrow, later, finish, recently, will,* and *now.*

Transliterators will delete words if they bring no additional meaning to the message.

> The thing that I want to emphasize most of all in this talk

Leave out *of all.*

> What is one of the big functions of our program?

Leave out *of the.*

Variations of the verb *to be*, are sometimes deleted, as in

> I am late.

> I was swimming.

But when the verb *to be* is meant as "become," transliterators use the sign BECOME.

> I want to be a firefighter when I grow up.

In Lou Fant's book *AMESLAN* (1972), he treats the verb *to be* in a special way. Fant uses the English example, "Hello! I'm glad to see you." From this sentence, he goes on to explain how to handle the verb *to be.*

> In AMESLAN, there is no sign for the verb 'to be.' If the sign <u>true</u> is substituted for 'am' in this sentence, the meaning is altered to 'I am truly glad to see you!' (p.2)

Fant replaces the verb *to be* with the sign TRUE. In *AMESLAN*, other English phrases are listed in which Fant suggests signing TRUE. These phrases and words include *it, is, am truly, sure, certain,* and *actually.*

SUMMARY

Transliterating is a complicated process that requires a tremendous amount of work. But transliterators are not glued to the English sentence verbatim as much as they are glued to the meaning. In the area of English sentence structure, the goal for the transliterator is to keep the English-based signing in an English sentence form.

Transliterators enhance their ability to go from English to English-based signing by learning more about English and ASL. Idiomatic expressions, a speech form that is peculiar within the usage of a given language, occur in every language. The way a word is used in one language may not be the same in another language in a literal translation. English is very idiomatic, and for this reason transliterators constantly make decisions about when to keep the idiomatic phrase, or when to find an equivalent meaning in order to retain clarity.

Transliterators use different tactics to add clarity to the message in English-based signing. They use additions, restructuring, and omissions. The use of addition adds clarity to the message by making the signed message more comprehensible to the consumer. Addition is done through cohesion, clarification, modality, adaptation, repetition, and reduplication.

Transliterators may need to restructure the signed message, which can occur in combination with any of the features of addition. Restructuring is done by replacing one grammatical structure with another. When a sentence is restructured, the mouthing of the English corresponds to the new, restructured form and not the original sentence structure from the source message.

Deletions are also part of the transliterating process. It is not always possible to keep up with the English output when transliterating, as English is produced at about 180 words per minute. True, the transliterator may be able to keep up with the full English message, but the signing would be so fast that the message would be lost. The transliterator needs to be pragmatic and make sure the message is clear.

ACTIVITIES

Exercise 3-1

Double meanings.

Read the following sentences and decide how to sign the underlined English words.

Example:

Are you <u>able</u> to come with me? He is a very <u>able</u> tennis player.

Are you able to come with me? He is a skilled tennis player

1. It was an <u>exhausting</u> trip. I have an <u>exhaustive</u> list.

2. Paper towels <u>absorb</u> water. The boy was <u>absorbed</u> in his game.

3. Give me an <u>account</u> of your trip. I want to open a bank <u>account</u>.

4. The dog <u>bared</u> his teeth. The house was quite <u>bare</u>.

5. A boy <u>becomes</u> a man. That red dress <u>becomes</u> her.

6. He kept a <u>clear</u> head. Our club <u>cleared</u> fifty dollars.

7. The bird is <u>dead</u>. There it is, <u>dead</u> ahead.

8. The cat was <u>out</u> all night. The fire is <u>out</u>.

9. I <u>passed</u> the test. Please <u>pass</u> me the salt.

10. In class we have 10 <u>rules</u>. Who <u>ruled</u> France in 1776?

11. Who is <u>running</u> the store? It snowed for two days <u>running</u>.

12. Write an original <u>sentence</u>. He was <u>sentenced</u> to 10 years.

13. The store <u>cut</u> their prices. <u>Cut</u> the paper in half.

14. Put the chair <u>by</u> the door. Let me know <u>by</u> phone.

Exercise 3-2

Restructure the English sentence into another English sentence. The goal is to keep the same meaning throughout this article.

Example:

The normal U.S. family has a father, mother, and children.

> The typical U.S. family is nuclear.
>
> The normal U.S. family has two parents and children.
>
> A mom, a dad, and kids make up the typical family in the United States.

1. What happens if a parent is removed from the home by death or divorce?

2. The effects of losing a mother are quite different to a family than the effects of losing the father.

3. A single father responsible for children often continues his working role.

4. He hires a caretaker to take over housekeeping and supervise his children.

5. When the father is missing from a family, the single mother usually works, and she may or may not hire a substitute caretaker.

6. The plight of single women with children seems most desperate and is increasing in frequency.

7. There are a number of severe problems associated with not having a father in the home.

8. The children can become excessively dependent on the mother.

9. So, what does a father mean to his family?

10. Boys learn how to be men by copying their fathers or other older males.

Exercise 3-3

Change the figure of speech underlined into a literal meaning while maintaining the same meaning.

Example:

Please <u>take up</u> the matter with your doctor.

Please talk with your doctor.

1. That factory <u>turns out</u> hundreds of cars a year.

2. When will this train <u>get to</u> San Francisco?

3. The patient <u>got better</u> after surgery.

4. Will you <u>look after</u> my house while I'm away?

5. The fire <u>died</u> with no one tending it.

6. Do you <u>go for</u> this kind of movie?

7. I <u>came across</u> the book I was looking for.

8. We need to <u>hold off</u> buying the car for a month.

9. My car <u>broke down</u> last week.

10. How much did the car <u>set you back</u>?

11. Can we <u>count on</u> your support?

12. What do the stars on the flag <u>stand for</u>?

Exercise 3-4

Add, restructure, paraphrase, or delete in order to clear up the concept.

Example:

Our organization tries to bring young and old together.

Our organization tries to bring young people and old people together.

1. Many women today are torn between responsibilities at home and on the job.

2. You should never waste any and all opportunities to practice.

3. If each and every person agrees, we will go ahead with our plan.

4. Three-quarters of all Americans own two televisions.

5. It is not necessarily wrong.

6. You can't go anywhere and not find a Starbucks.

7. You will be in hot water if you do that.

8. He was a potato couch.

9. Don't count your chickens before they're hatched.

Exercise 3-5

Put the following sentences into idiomatic English.

Example:

Just get that out of your head.

Just get that out of your mind.

1. Put on your socks and shoes.

2. Please put out the spoons, forks, and knives.

3. Here comes the future wife.

4. Is that your last answer?

5. I like my men tall, dark, and strong.

6. The three smart men from the East followed the Star of Bethlehem.

7. I love the flag, the old white, red, and blue.

8. I won't buy it if it says "Manufactured in China."

9. OK, girls and boys, today we study the three R's: writing, 'rithmetic, and reading.

■■■ CHAPTER 4

Mouth Movements

ORAL TRANSLITERATORS

Transliterators use the feature of mouth movements from English when providing an English-based interpretation. Transliterators use this visual feature to portray English words on the lips.

Interpreters who perform oral transliterating, or oral interpreting, are trained to listen to the spoken English message and rephrase the message into a readable speech form. For oral transliterators, "it is critical to understand the task of speech reading and all of the challenges to be met therein" (RSA Federal Interpreter Training Center, 1995, pp. 5A-5). Oral transliterating is a separate skill from what is expected of a sign language transliterator, as it requires intense and specialized training. This book will not look at the task of oral transliterating, but people interested in oral transliteration can contact the A. G. Bell Association for the Deaf, Inc., in Washington, D.C.

DOES MOUTHING ENGLISH MEAN SIM-COM?

The ability to hear, sign, and speak English at the same time is referred to as *simultaneous communication*, or *sim-com*. When transliterators move their mouths in order to show the English words, and sign at the same time, this should not be considered sim-com. The person performing sim-com is focusing more on the English language than on the sign language, because they are receiving auditory feedback. It has been noted that when sim-com is used, features pertaining to ASL, such as lexical choice, head and body shifting, facial markers, and use of space, which are critical in relaying a visual message, are often lost (Humphrey & Alcorn, 1995).

This dropping of ASL features happens because when receiving auditory feedback, the hearing person believes the communication has been clear. Deaf people, however, note that when a hearing person signs and talks at the same time, signs are omitted, semantically incorrect signs are used, signs are slurred, and there are deleted ASL non-markers, while non-manual behaviors of English are used, all of which results in the message being skewed.

When transliterators move their lips silently to mouth English while signing in an English word order, there is no auditory feedback. The transliterator is aware of what does and does not make sense in a visual target language and is not dependent on the auditory English. The primary focus is on having the message make sense, and transliterators put meaning above form in their output.

MOUTH MOVEMENTS

When transliterators present English on their lips, it is referred to as "mouthing." However, there is more to transliterating than just adding mouth movements to an interpretation. First, a few facts on this aspect of English speech (RSA Federal Interpreter Training Center, 1995):

The English language has 28 different mouth shapes and 38 to 43 different sounds (depending on accent).

60 to 70% of isolated speech sounds are produced within the mouth and are not visible on the lips.

Ordinary speech averages 13 sounds per second, while the eye is capable of seeing only 8-10 sounds per second.

When mouthing English words, the lips should take on a natural presentation. Transliterators should face the consumer(s), and should not exaggerate their mouth movements, smack their lips, or whisper. There should be no distracting habits such as random head movements. Transliterators should keep their hands from blocking the mouth, especially when fingerspelling.

Not all English words have a literal sign equivalent, and there are times when a specific sign can be recoded into more than one English word. Because of this ambiguity in the manual mode, mouthing is used to indicate which English word is being transliterated. In this case, transliterators mouth the word because "the mouthing serves to distinguish the intended meaning of the manual sign"(Winston, 1989, p. 160). In the sentence,

> The teacher that spoke was brilliant

the transliterator mouths *brilliant* and signs SMART. While in the sentence,

> The plan corresponds with our yearly goals

transliterators can sign RELATE and mouth *corresponds*. In both sentences, a specific English word is mouthed to correspond with a specific sign.

If, for clarity, the transliterator has restructured the sentence, or taken the sentence from two negatives in English to a positive statement in sign language, then she mouths the new restructured English sentence.

FINGERSPELLING FOR CLARITY

When a transliterator uses a sign that does not normally correspond with the English word, simply mouthing the word and picking a sign that has multiple meanings may not be clearly understood by the consumer. In this case, the transliterator would fingerspell the English word and then provide the sign chosen for the ASL equivalent. For example, assume the transliterator encounters the following sentence:

We need to look at the variables involved in this project.

One choice transliterators can use is the sign VARIOUS. If this is the choice, then the transliterator fingerspells V-A-R-I-A-B-L-E-S, signs VARIOUS, and mouths the word *variables* to demonstrate that the sign VARIOUS will now represent the English word *variable* in this context. The transliterator can decide to do the sign first and then fingerspell the word, or fingerspell the word and then produce the sign. Either way is acceptable. The choice is between you and the consumer. In another example,

We need to advocate for the rights of children

if the transliterator has determined that the word *advocate* is as critical to the message as the meaning, then she could sign SUPPORT and fingerspell A-D-V-O-C-A-T-E to demonstrate that the sign SUPPORT will represent this particular English word for this context.

CHANGING ENGLISH WORDS THAT SHOW SOUND-RELATED CONCEPTS

There are times when a transliterator encounters an English word that is sound-related and difficult to present in sign language except through fingerspelling. These words are called onomatopoeias. Examples are *plop, meow, crack*, and *ding-dong*. A study conducted by Susan A. Mather in 1989 called "Visually Oriented Teaching Strategies" looked at teaching strategies used with Deaf preschool children. One area of focus was how native signers changed English words to show sound-related concepts in signs.

Mather's study involves the story "Three Little Kittens." When looking at how native and non-native signers handled the word *meow* from the story, it was noted that "the native signer translates the word as CRY (in the sense of 'whimper')" (Mather, 1989, p. 184). This translation was consistent with the intended meaning. In an English-based sign language, as well as ASL, there is no established sign for *meow*. As the native signer continued to sign, "she changes her choice of mouthing from 'Cry' to 'Meow' and signs while meowing orally" (Mather, 1989, p. 185).

As with native signers, the transliterator strives to maintain meaning and translates the word to a sign that is consistent with the intended meaning while mouthing the English word. With the sentence,

The dog was growling at the man

the transliterator signs a modified version of BARK. The transliterator mouths *growl* if the English word is important or mouths *bark* if the meaning is important.

SUMMARY

The goal of mouthing during transliterating is to allow the consumer to see what is being said in English by using a visual feature of English, the movement of the lips. Mouthing while transliterating is not the same as simultaneous-communication (sim-com). Sim-com is speaking out loud while signing. Because of the auditory feedback during sim-com, signs and ASL features tend to be dropped. Transliterators do mouth the words while signing, but do not vocalize the words; therefore, they do not have to deal with auditory feedback.

The English language has 28 different mouth shapes and 38 to 43 different sounds. Only 30 to 40% of these sounds are visible, as 60 to 70% of isolated speech sounds are produced within the mouth. Ordinary speech averages 13 sounds per second, while the eye is capable of seeing only 8 to 10 sounds per second.

Mouthing of English words should be presented as naturally as possible, neither exaggerating the lips nor whispering. Transliterators should avoid blocking the mouth with signs and fingerspelling. When they hear an English word and place it with a sign that is not normally glossed with the English word choice, they can mouth the English speaker's word choice. When a sentence is restructured during transliterating, the transliterator mouths the new restructured English sentence.

When a sign is being used that represents a specific English word, the transliterator either fingerspells the English word, then provides the equivalent sign choice, or provides the equivalent sign, then fingerspells the English word. Words that are sound-related will be transliterated to the intended meaning while mouthing the word that is presented in English.

ACTIVITIES

Activity 4-1

Practice transliterating the sentences. Sign the appropriate sign for the underlined word while mouthing the stated English word.

Example:

You can't <u>evade</u> your responsibility.

    You can't avoid your responsibility.

1. <u>Every now and then,</u> I like to go to the mountains.

2. <u>Every Monday</u> night I have class.

3. Let's <u>suppose </u>you win the lottery? What would you buy?

4. My mother <u>used to </u>work in Canada.

5. Are you <u>dissatisfied</u> with your work?

6. I need <u>assistance</u> with my project.

7. She graduated <u>already</u>.

8. What is the <u>purpose</u> for the meeting?

9. They <u>declared</u> the winner this morning.

10. There is a <u>possibility</u> of rain this evening.

11. We need to <u>make up</u> an original story for class.

12. They seemed to have the <u>innate</u> ability to succeed.

13. I was really <u>amazed.</u>

Activity 4-2

Practice transliterating the sentences. Create a sign for, or a way to convey, the underlined word.

1. The bird <u>chirped</u> in the trees.

2. The water <u>gurgled</u> over the rocks.

3. The snake <u>hissed</u> as it slithered.

4. The cat <u>purred</u> its contentment.

5. The room was silent except for the <u>tick-tock</u> of the clock.

6. The water from the faucet, the constant <u>plop, plop</u>, drove her crazy.

7. The <u>tinkling</u> of the wind chimes was pleasant.

8. The guns went off, <u>bang, bang.</u>

9. The door <u>creaked</u> open.

■■ CHAPTER 5

Fingerspelling

THE PURPOSE OF FINGERSPELLING

Fingerspelling is used primarily in ASL to represent proper nouns, specific terms, English words that do not have an ASL lexical equivalent, and technical terms. "In everyday signing, fingerspelled words appear as frequently as 7-10% of the overall vocabulary" (Padden, 1991). Words that are fingerspelled include names, abbreviations, and items not found in the ASL lexicon (Battison, 1978). Transliterators have to make decisions on what is and is not fingerspelled during their work, and how to present that word during the rest of the transliteration. There are six ways fingerspelled words can be handled: lexicalized signs, replacing fingerspelled words with classifiers, replacing fingerspelled words with signs, abbreviations, name signs, and initialized signs.

METHODS OF FINGERSPELLING

Lexicalized Fingerspelling

Lexicalized fingerspelled words, also known as *loan signs*, are "words that are fingerspelled but undergo a systemic, phonological, morphological and semantic change" (Battison, 1978). Lexicalized fingerspelled words are fingerspelled words that eventually become a part of the ASL lexicon. Some words that have already become part of the standard ASL lexicon, whether they are interpreted or transliterated, are BACK, BUS, WHAT, ALL, STYLE, and BANK. Some characteristics of lexicalized signs are letter deletion, special movement, and palm orientation (Battison, 1978).

Letter deletion. Letter deletion happens when a fingerspelled word, such as *back*, has letters deleted. Instead of fingerspelling B-A-C-K, the word is lexicalized by signing B-C-K.

Special movement. Fingerspelled words normally have no movement other than the movement caused by the change from one letter to another. Lexicalized words have a special movement incorporated into them. An example of this characteristic is the word *early*, which has a circular movement.

Palm orientation. Fingerspelled words are produced with the palm facing away from the signer. Lexicalized signs sometimes include a change of palm orientation, as in the word JOB. The "J" is produced palm forward, but the "B" ends the word with the palm facing the signer.

Lexicalized signs can incorporate one or more of the above parameters.

Replacing Fingerspelled Words with Classifiers

Classifiers (CL:s) are handshapes that represent a noun and indicate the location and possible actions of that noun (Baker & Cokely, 1980). Some CL:s are like pronouns because they represent a noun. For this reason, a CL: needs the noun to be clearly stated. CL:s may also function as verbs. In some situations, a CL: is a size and shape specifier (SASS).

When replacing a fingerspelled noun with a CL:, the transliterator can fingerspell the word, then replace it with a CL: or SASS. Once the CL: or SASS has replaced the fingerspelled word, the transliterator continues to use the CL: or SASS to represent that English word. In some cases, the English word itself is more important than the actual concept. If this is the case, then the transliterator increases the number of times the word is fingerspelled while alternating the fingerspelled word with the CL: or SASS.

The following two examples show how a transliterator can replace the fingerspelled word with a CL:

Birds, every year, will migrate.

In this sentence the transliterator fingerspells M-I-G-R-A-T-E and then replaces it with 2 open 5 handshapes, palms down, moving through the air. Repeat the fingerspelled word and add the CL: until it is clear that the CL: represents the fingerspelled word M-I-G-R-A-T-E.

We want to pass a bill to regulate billboards.

The word *billboard* is first fingerspelled and then replaced by a 2 handed L-handshape. Again, the transliterator does not make the transition from fingerspelling to CL: immediately, but fingerspells the word often enough so the consumer relates the fingerspelled word with the CL:.

Replacing Fingerspelled Words with Signs

What if a fingerspelled word cannot be replaced by a classifier? Within all languages there are a variety of ways that words express meaning, and a word may not only have a primary meaning, but may also have secondary meanings or figurative meanings (Larson, 1984). When the use of a classifier is not possible, a fingerspelled word could be replaced with a sign that is semantically correct though not normally associated with the fingerspelled word.

The process of replacing a fingerspelled word with an untypical ASL sign requires *flagging*. Davis (1989) noted that a fingerspelled word is often flagged with an ASL lexical marker, which could be a demonstrative pronoun, a quotation mark, or a multi-meaning ASL sign. Flagging a fingerspelled word involves first fingerspelling the word, followed immediately by the sign intended to replace the fingerspelling. This is similar to the process of identifying a noun, then introducing a classifier to represent that noun.

An example of flagging occurred in a setting in which the English word *habitat* came up often. When the transliterator realized *habitat* would be used frequently during the presentation, she fingerspelled H-A-B-I-T-A-T, then immediately signed HOME. The transliterator flagged *habitat* with the sign HOME to show that the sign would afterwards take the place of fingerspelling word.

Abbreviations

Within a specific context, the words that are abbreviated in an English-based sign language are the same words abbreviated in English. Words often abbreviated are state and capital names, and acronyms of organizations, post-secondary facilities for the Deaf, and local agency names (Wells, 1983). But there are also abbreviations found in different fields and businesses.

English words that can be abbreviated are first fingerspelled and then given the accepted acronym or abbreviation to represent them. For example, if one were in a chemistry class, the chemical elements from the Periodic Table are replaced with their appropriate nomenclature. An "H" represents hydrogen and an "O" represents oxygen. The transliterator would need to know which elements are not represented by their first letter in the Periodic Table, such as iron, which is represented by "Fe," or sodium, which is represented by "Na" (Phillips, 1983).

Warning: Do not make up an abbreviation! A problem might occur, as in a medical situation. Let us say a transliterator abbreviates a term in a way that is not customary in the medical field. The next transliterator gets information from the consumer, who in discussing his or her medical problem, uses the first transliterator's incorrect abbreviation. The abbreviation is then used by the current transliterator to the doctor, who cannot use it to clarify the medical problem. Do the research and make sure the abbreviation is appropriate for the setting.

Name Signs

Name signs fall under two basic categories: descriptive and arbitrary (Supalla, 1992). A Descriptive Name Sign (DNS) refers to a physical characteristic used to identify a person. An Arbitrary Name Sign (ANS) follows a system that is standardized and widely used across the United States. In a study in which 450 ASL name signs were collected, only 19 percent fell under the DNS category (Meadow, 1977).

Names may come up repeatedly during lectures. Some famous people, such as Abraham Lincoln, Hitler, and George Washington, already have name signs. For people that do not have name signs, one option is representing the name with a shaking letter; however, transliterators have other choices as well when creating names signs. Sam Supalla's book *The Book of Name Signs: Naming in American Sign Language* (1992) is quite helpful and an excellent resource for name signs.

Not every name that occurs during transliteration requires a name sign. If a name is short, such as *Sue*, or flows easily, such as *Barry*, then it is easier to fingerspell the name than to create a name sign. But there are situations in which the transliterator will choose to use name signs.

Sometimes a transliterator must contrast two people, such as in a college literature class that is discussing a Shakespearean play. In the play "Midsummer Night's Dream," there are two main female characters, Hermia and Helena. When the teacher compares the two characters, the transliterator can represent these names with Arbitrary Names Signs.

The Book of Name Signs lists three types of ANS:

ANS in Neutral Space. The first letter of the name is placed in front of the transliterator.

ANS with Single Location on Body. Take the first letter of the name and place it on a location on the body. The movement for contact is repeated. The areas that can be used include, but are not limited to, the forehead, the side of the mouth, and over the heart.

ANS with Dual Locations of Body. The first letter of the name is used with two locations on the body. The movements that can be used include, but are not limited to, movement from the chin to the chest, and from the forehead to the chin.

According to Supalla's book, names of family members usually stay together in the same area. All the brothers' and sisters' names are on the chin, on the forehead, on the chest, or wherever the parents have chosen to represent their family.

Name signs that a transliterator creates should only be thought of as context- and topic-related. Once the transliterator is no longer in the same context or on the same topic, any name sign created would no longer be valid.

Initialized Signs

Initialized signs represent an English word based on a traditional sign. Examples are the words *group, family,* and *team*. When the initialized signs FAMILY or TEAM are used, the base sign, a "bent 5" to represent a group of people, is chosen because it semantically relates to the new concept (Klima & Bellugi, 1979). Everything about each of the signs (location, movement, and place of articulation) is the same except the handshape, which adapts to reflect the first initial of the English word it represents.

So when does one initialize a sign? "Initialization is one of the most productive of word-building processes in ASL, used widely for technical or professional purposes" (Padden, 1998). Transliterators should be aware of how Deaf adults use initialization. What transliterators should avoid is what I call "the shaking C." There are signs that take the first letter of the word and are shaken in neutral space, such as shaking the letter "I" for *insurance*. "The shaking C" happens when a transliterator has no sign to replace the fingerspelled word, does not want to keep fingerspelling the word, is not aware of other alternatives to use, and thus simply takes the first letter of the word and shakes it in neutral space.

The biggest problem with "the shaking C" becomes apparent if you imagine yourself as the next transliterator. There you are with a Deaf consumer. During the appointment, the consumer shakes a letter because the previous transliterator did it, and you are supposed to be able to voice the appropriate English word. It is nearly impossible to guess what word is represented by "the shaking C," which could mean Connie, cucumber, conservative, or any other word that begins with the letter "C." For this reason, strive to use only established initialized signs while transliterating or use the other approaches discussed, such as replacing the fingerspelled word with a classifier.

Some initialized signs are widely used among Deaf adults, while others are used primarily by consumers in a specific setting. Initialized signs used at work or in a classroom may be familiar to any Deaf person in that particular environment, but may not be familiar to consumers outside of that job or class.

SUMMARY

Fingerspelling, as part of ASL, is used to represent proper nouns, words that do not have signed lexical equivalents, and technical terms and is, therefore, part of the transliterating task. Fingerspelling can be handled in a variety of ways. One way is to use lexicalized fingerspelling for words that have become part of the ASL lexicon. Lexicalized fingerspelling includes such words as BACK, BUS, STYLE, and BANK. Characteristics of lexicalized signs are letter deletion, special movement, and palm orientation.

Classifiers (CL:s) and size and shape specifiers (SASS) can be used to replace fingerspelled words. This replacement is not done immediately. During transliterating there is a transition from the fingerspelled word to the classifier. This process may be repeated with three or four fingerspelled words to make sure the classifier is identified as representing the fingerspelled word.

A fingerspelled word can also be replaced with a sign. The process of replacing a fingerspelled word with a sign is similar to the process of identifying a noun, then introducing a classifier to represent that noun. Once a word has been given a sign, the fingerspelled word can be replaced by that sign for the remainder of the transliterating.

Abbreviated words are common in business, technical, or educational settings, and transliterators should avail themselves of the standard abbreviations used in the settings in which they are working.

Name signs are another option. Name signs are either descriptive (created to denote a physical characteristic to describe the person) or arbitrary (standardized signs that are used across the United States). Various well-known individuals have name signs already established, and these should be used. Name signs that are created by the transliterator should be considered context-specific and topic-specific.

Initialized signs represent English words but are based on traditional signs. Initialized signs should be signs already used by Deaf adults. If an initialized sign is created, then that sign should remain in that specific context and not be used in another setting without being properly established.

ACTIVITIES

Activity 5-1

Decide how you would handle the fingerspelling of the underlined words.

1. I belong to the <u>League</u> of Women Voters.

2. The doctor told me I need to decrease my <u>cholesterol</u>.

3. Are you a member of the <u>Registry of Interpreters for the Deaf</u>?

4. We will discuss <u>fiscal year</u> 1997-1998.

5. Water is made up of <u>two parts hydrogen</u> and <u>one part oxygen</u>.

6. We will discuss <u>classifiers</u> and their use in sign language.

7. I am visiting <u>New Jersey</u> this summer.

8. He graduated from the <u>National Technical Institute for the Deaf</u>.

Activity 5-2

Decide how you would replace the underlined words with a classifier.

Practice 1:

Earth is the third planet from the sun and the fifth largest of the planets in this Solar System. The earth is considered to consist of four parts. In the middle of the earth is the <u>inner core</u>. This inner core looks like a ball, surrounded by the rest of the earth. The next layer is called the <u>outer core</u>. This section is 1,380 miles thick and surrounds the inner core. The next layer is called the <u>mantle</u>. The mantle is 1,800 miles thick, solid, and with a density that increases with depth. The outer part of the earth is called the <u>crust</u>. Only 25 miles deep, the crust is where life is sustained.

Practice 2:

Let us now look at the next area of study, which is graphing. Sometimes we use a graph that uses <u>rows</u> and <u>columns</u>. Who knows the difference between a row and a column? Right, the row goes from left to right, and the column from top to bottom. One way to remember this is to think of plants. Plants are grown in rows. The rows of plants are from left to right and in straight lines. Now, do any of you remember old buildings? They have front porches. The things that hold up those porches are called columns. These columns go up and down.

Activity 5-3

First, decide which words would be fingerspelled. Second, decide how you would handle the fingerspelled words. Are the words fingerspelled, flagged, or replaced with a CL?

Welcome to Basic Mechanics 101A. I know most of you are here to learn how to work on cars, but we will start off a bit more elementary. This morning we will be looking at bicycles and how to conduct simple repairs. You will notice in the illustration that the basic frame of the bike is referred to as a tube. You have the top tube, the head tube, the down tube, and the seat tube, which is directly below the seat. The piece of the frame that holds the front tire is called a fork, while the back two pieces holding the rear tire are called the seat stay and the chain stay. There are over 20 parts labeled in the diagram in your book and you should learn all of them.

Let's talk a bit about tools. There are just a few basic tools that are essential to bike repair. First, buy a good crescent wrench. There is an illustration on the board for those who are not familiar with it. To test the wrench, open the adjustable jaw and see if it moves up and down. Second, buy a screwdriver. Find one with a thin blade end. The tip should be 1/4 inch wide. Third, get a cable clipper. The best is a heavy duty bicycle cable clipper that grabs the cable in a diamond shaped hole and shears it off clean. And finally, get a hammer. Any simple small hammer is fine. These four tools are absolutely essential for bike repair.

Activity 5-4

First, decide which words would be fingerspelled. Second, decide how you would handle the fingerspelled words.

Many people claim that by providing minorities with special privileges, such as Affirmative Action, the country experiences a decline in unity and values. The claim is that by giving preference to minorities in hiring, education, and government contracts, the American ideals of equal opportunity and justice are betrayed. Also, the unity of the country is weakened, as one racial group is pitted against the other. But this is not the case. By providing minorities with special attention and privileges, the American values of equal opportunity, equal justice, and general equality are enhanced, and the country is unified in the long run.

The American nation was founded on the ideals of liberty, justice, freedom, and equal opportunity. However, from the very beginning it was obvious some people were more free, had more opportunities, and received more justice and liberties than others were. Almost all blacks were enslaved, women could not vote, and non-whites were denied participation in the American system and kept in the state of internal colonialism.

This situation continued well into the 20th century, even after slavery was abolished and women given the right to vote. During the civil rights era, special government programs were created that tried to eliminate this contradiction and level the playing field for people of all races, by giving preferences to minorities. This would include Affirmative Action and integration. These programs corrected past wrongs and prevented them from continuing.

■■ CHAPTER 6

Use of Space

English and ASL are two separate languages with different grammatical identities. English is a language that is auditory and vocal, and is expressed orally by making a series of sound patterns organized sequentially (Humphrey & Alcorn, 1995). ASL is a language based on visual perception and conveyance (Baker & Cokely, 1980).

Although transliterators do not work between two distinct languages, they do work between an auditory and vocal language and a visual language. Because of this, transliterators need to be aware of the grammatical differences between the modes of these two languages. ASL, a visual language, is communicated through a visual modality. One area used effectively by transliterators to enhance meaning is the use of space, which adds clarity to information by locating objects and entities in the signing space. Areas that will be discussed within the use of space are *direct address, subject-object agreement, non-manual markers, listing,* and *comparisons.*

DIRECT ADDRESS

There are two kinds of grammatical forms that encode speech events: direct and indirect address (Larson, 1984). Direct address, in ASL, is defined as acting out the role of the character using direct dialogue (Marron, 1999). An example of direct address is when a signer conveys a situation such as a teacher talking with a student and portrays the teacher and student by using body shifts, changes in eye gaze, and different demeanors to represent each person. Direct address is also known as "role-shifting."

When a language has both direct and indirect address, such as English, there is usually a special function for each (Larson, 1984). In English, direct address occurs when the person speaking takes on the role of someone else and uses an informal register. English speakers, when taking on the role of a character, will do so most often when telling stories and jokes and when speaking to children.

Direct address in English is used less frequently than in ASL, as direct address in ASL occurs not only in storytelling but also in everyday discourse and is used in both formal and informal registers. If the English sentence is,

Mother told Sue she wanted her to clean the house

transliterators use direct address and signs MOTHER + TOLD + S U E + I + WANT + YOU + CLEAN + HOUSE. Note that the sentence has been restructured to handle the direct address, but the restructured sentence still follows English word order.

Transliterators need to take note of the function of direct address. When going from a signed language to English, do not use direct address if it is inappropriate. For example, if a Deaf man signs that a Deaf woman told him,

MY + INTERPRETER + GOOD

and the Deaf man signed this statement using direct address, the transliterator would say, "I met a Deaf woman and she told me her interpreter was good," as opposed to "I met a Deaf woman and she told me my interpreter was good." The sign MY denotes a direct address because the signer was referring to a comment made by another person and not himself. The MY is changed into the English *her* to clarify that the person talking is referring to a third person.

SUBJECT-OBJECT AGREEMENT

ASL, being a three-dimensional language, uses the area around the signer to give information that assists in understanding. "Additionally, body and facial agreement must complement the composite" (Lawrence, 1995, p. 210). The space close to and in front of the transliterator is considered "first person." The location of the person the signer is talking with is "second person." The spatial location of other people, places, or things is "third person" (Baker & Cokely, 1982). By using these locations, the transliterator is clear when using verbs that utilize and depend on spatial location. Take the sentence below:

John gave me the book.

In this sentence, the verb *gave* would move from the space designated for John toward the transliterator, representing "me." But if the sentence is changed to,

I gave John the book

the verb *gave* would move from the transliterator, "I," out to the space designated for John. Grammatically, the transliterator is still following English, not ASL, but the verb is modulated to move in a clear direction depending on who did the giving. Transliterators use the signing space around them to establish locations for objects, people, and entities in the signing space. After establishing a location, transliterators use that referent to refer back to the object. In the example,

I live in California and my mom lives in New York. I plan to fly out to visit her next summer.

the transliterator, maintaining the English word order, would modulate the verb *to fly* to move from the area for first person, to where "mom" is set up in New York. Subject-object agreement can, however, become complicated, as we see in this next example:

The teacher has to monitor the reading level of her students. When that student is assisted at home, studies have shown reading levels improve.

The transliterator must establish the teacher monitoring the reading level of her students at one location (the school) and the student reading in two locations (the school and the home). By using space to set up the school and the home, these two locations are clearly established. Following this, the transliterator can show the concept that by being assisted at home, the student will improve his or her reading level at school. If space is not used, the consumer might think the teacher is assisting the student in the home.

NON-MANUAL MARKERS

Signers form adjectives in ASL by using non-manual markers, which are also grammatical markers that use the face and body to convey information. Facial non-manual markers are grammatical signals on the face that show whether a sentence is a question, what type of question it is, whether it is a negative statement, and so forth (Baker & Cokely, 1982).

A facial non-manual marker is used if someone says they were driving in "heavy traffic." In this case the face would have puffed cheeks and the eyes would squint. If the person were driving in "light traffic," the face would have pouty lips and the eyes would be more open. For transliterators to convey the meaning of either "light traffic" or "heavy traffic," they still need to place the English words *light traffic* or *heavy traffic* on their mouths, but the rest of the face takes on the non-manual markers found in ASL.

Transliterators might think they should not use non-manual markers, as these non-manual markers are not used by English speakers. Yet, if the transliterator does not use facial markers, the visual language will lose meaning because they are necessary for appropriate and accurate transliteration. Without non-manual facial markers, the transliteration becomes monotone. Facial markers add clarity to the message and enhance meaning that may not be represented by a literal recoding of English into manual signs.

Body non-manual markers are grammatical markers that show the relationships between subjects and objects. They are used for characterizations and sentence markers, such as conditional topic sentences (Baker & Cokely, 1982). By including body non-manual markers, transliterators mark separation of clauses, topic shifts, and sentence markers.

If appropriate markers are not used, the transliterator is, in essence, using run-on sentences. Not only is this boring, but meaning is lost. Without these markers, it would be like reading the following without punctuation:

> I am going to the store will you go with me I want to buy a dress if it is not too late we can also stop at the bank but we can't if Suzy doesn't get here soon I wonder if my mom will call oh here she is now goodbye.

Some facial and body non-manual markers transliterators should use are listed below:

Head nod. Head nods show the topic is over and the speaker is moving on to a new topic. Head nods are also used in conditional sentences.

Eye gaze. Eye gaze shows where the topic of discussion is going, is a cue for fingerspelling and referents, and signals a change in the speaker's role. Eye gaze also shows authority or condescension by either looking up or down. Direct address eye gaze is used during role shift.

Body shift. Body shifts are used for direct address or to show a comparison.

LISTING AND COMPARISONS

Transliterators following English word order still need to set up items spatially in order to make the most sense visually. Spatial referencing uses the space around the signer to establish a person or place and is necessary when listing or comparing (Baker & Cokely, 1982).

The term *listing* is used when items are grouped together. Transliterators indicate that items are a list by using a numbering system on their non-dominant hand or by placing items in the same area spatially. Listing would use a numbering system in the sentence,

> I am taking history, math, and English in college.

In this sentence the transliterator can sign I + TAKE UP + FIRST + HISTORY + SECOND + MATH + THIRD + ENGLISH +IN + COLLEGE.

Listing also includes the idea of placement. The above example can be done without a numbering system: simply sign HISTORY, MATH, and ENGLISH in the same space. Or when a text contains two people who are mentioned as doing the same thing, these two people can be placed in the same area.

> Karen and Joe work with me.

Since Karen and Joe are mentioned as doing the same thing and are not being compared, they can be set up spatially together on either the right or left side of the transliterator.

When a text has two items that are to be compared, those items are set up on the left and right space in front of the transliterator. Setting up referents in space to show a comparison is used in a sentence that begins with,

> The difference between freshmen and seniors is…

Transliterators set up *freshmen* spatially to one side and *seniors* on the other side. For the remainder of the text, by using the pronominalizations of these two groups, the transliterator can reference all attributes and characteristics of each group in the appropriate space.

SUMMARY

Use of space is a conscious decision made by the transliterator to add clarity to the signed message. An English-based sign language is a visual mode and therefore uses the grammatical features of direct address, non-manual markers, subject-object agreement, and listing and comparisons. By using these grammatical features of ASL, transliterators can add clarity to the message and still retain English word order. These features do not take away from the English message, but rather add to the English-based sign language message.

Direct address is used more often in ASL than in English. English tends to use direct address when telling stories and jokes or when speaking to children and is used in a more informal register. Direct address in ASL is used in all areas of discourse, in both formal and informal registers. When voicing from an English-based sign language to English, the transliterator should not use direct address when it is not appropriate to do so.

Non-manual markers are grammatical markers that use the face and body to convey information. Facial non-manual markers are grammatical signals on the face used for conditional and topic/comment sentences and for questions. Without these markers, transliterators convey information in run-on sentences, which are also monotone.

Body non-manual markers are grammatical markers that show relationships between subjects and objects and are also used as sentence markers. Subject-object agreement is used because ASL is a three-dimensional language. Transliterators use subject-object agreement and the area around them to assist the consumer in understanding the message. Some non-manual markers that transliterators use include the head nod, used to show topic/comment and conditional sentences; eye gaze, used to indicate the direction of discussion, to cue for fingerspelling, or to signal a change in the speaker's role; and body shifts, used for direct address and to show comparison.

Transliterators use space for listing and comparing items. Listing is used when similar items are grouped together, and the same space can be utilized. When comparing two different items, each item is set up on a different side of the transliterator and compared. All attributes and characteristics of each item are then referenced to the appropriate space. With the use of space, transliterators are able to convey the original spoken meaning without losing English grammar.

ACTIVITIES

Activity 6-1

Identify when to list and when to compare in the story. In pairs, practice transliterating the story.

> Jim and Sheila were right about each other. They are different. Yet they were able to salvage their marriage after they were shown how all of us fall into one of four basic personality classifications. With this knowledge, Jim and Sheila learned to be more flexible in their differences.
>
> The theory utilized here was established by Carl Jung. He wrote that in human communication, people are divided into four distinctive behavioral categories. People who belong to the same behavioral category tend to wear the same kind of clothes, have the same kind of friends, see the world in the same way, and so on.
>
> But the important point of the four categories is how they affect communication style. If our communication styles are similar, we think alike, enjoy the same kinds of activities, and express ideas in the same way. But if our styles are different, we may have a difficult time fully understanding each other. There are four basic communicating styles: the thinker, the feeler, the intuitor, and the sensor.
>
> The "thinker" is organized, structured, and always searches for facts. He seldom makes quick, unprepared decisions. But once having made a decision, he will stick with it. The "thinker" has a conservative look, an orderly life, and an accurate checkbook. On the negative side, he can get too engrossed in details and be rigid and boring. Only about one in every four Americans is in this category. They include engineers, computer specialists, lawyers, accountants, and teachers.
>
> The second classification is called the "feeler." The "feeler" is emotional and known for his love of people, adventure, and involvement. For this group, the biggest problem is boredom. They are always trying new things. "Feelers" tend to enjoy pleasing themselves. They like bright styles and bright colors. But for persons with other communication styles, the "feeler" can be a real nuisance—unpredictable, with a "don't care," "free-spirit" attitude. Some experts estimate that 25% of our population are "feelers." They turn up in such fields as acting, sales, writing, and nursing.
>
> The third class is the "intuitor." They are imaginative and enjoy mind-testing games. The technical details of life often bore them or are just

forgotten. People of other styles are easily irritated by the "intuitor" because she gets impatient with anyone who doesn't see the immediate value of her ideas. She is usually rigid, uncompromising, and impractical. There are not many "intuitors," only about one person in ten. They are inventors, scientists, and researchers.

The last group is the "sensor." The "sensor" is easy to spot. They make up about 40% of the American population. The "sensor" enjoys the thrill of the chase, plus a fast payoff. Her answer to feelings of doubt or anxiety is to do something. Many business executives in America are "sensors" and so are many of our best athletes. The "sensor" tends to give and demand total loyalty. If she fails, she tends to blame others for not being as aggressive as she is.

Jim was a "thinker," while Sheila was a "feeler." After they understood how each other communicated and dealt with issues, they were able to better handle any conflicts that arose in their marriage.

■■ CHAPTER 7

Nouns, Verbs, and Pronouns

MEANING VS. FORM

Interpreters are taught to drop form and look for the meaning behind the English words. When an interpreter is asked to transliterate, one might assume that a sign that represents a particular word or concept in ASL would represent the same word or concept in an English-based sign language. The difficulty with this is that when staying close to the English structure, the sign choice is more influenced by the spoken English word than the meaning of the English word. When staying within English word order, using appropriate signs, and often using a shorter processing time, transliterators have to quickly be aware of alternative meanings of English words and which choice best fits the transliteration.

Transliterators must look for the correct meaning behind the word. If a transliterator heard the statement "they got there," the conceptually accurate transliteration for *got* would be the sign ARRIVE instead of the sign GOT. If the transliterator heard "the letter finally came," the sign choice for *finally* would not be the sign LAST, but rather the sign SUCCESS. Surface meaning alone cannot be taken into account by the transliterator, as there may be several meanings embedded in one word. If you were to look up the word *set,* you would find it has 74 definitions (Morris, 1980).

One example of a problem that can arise if the transliterator only looks at surface meaning is the following sentence from a hymn:

> Give me your love that I may serve you.

If the transliterator signs the English word *may* as MAYBE instead of the sign CAN, the sentence is changed from a positive, forward movement to a noncommittal statement. Transliterators must keep in mind that there are two goals: 1) to produce an English-based sign language, and 2) to make sense to the consumer. Sometimes these two goals conflict. When there is a conflict, the second goal, to make sense, takes precedence.

If one must deviate from the original English, the goal of the transliterator is to have the modified signed version remain as close as possible to the English structured form and produce a signed sentence that still follows English word order. However, the signed version might not be in the English word order that was originally produced.

PARTS OF SPEECH AND HOW THEY AFFECT TRANSLITERATING

The meaning of a word sometimes depends on the word's part of speech. In the sentence *I teach biology*, the word *teach* is a verb. When the suffix *er* is added to the word *teach*, as in *I am a teacher*, the word *teacher* is a noun. The meaning of the word is not only imbedded in the root word, but also in the suffix. This may seem obvious in the above example, but there are situations when this is not as clear.

The following sentences,

> I cook dinner every night

> I work as a cook

both contain the work *cook*. In the first statement, *cook* is a verb; in the second statement, *cook* is a noun. For clearer understanding by the consumer, the agent sign ER is added to the sign COOK in the second sentence to show the meaning is a person who cooks. If someone were talking about the field of interpreting and said,

> We have different membership levels for professionals in our field

the sign PROFESSIONAL for the word *professionals* is not enough. The English word *professional* can be either an adjective or a noun. In this sentence, the word *professionals* serves as a noun. Transliterators could sign INTERPRETERS to delineate between the adjective and the noun, or sign PROFESSIONAL + PEOPLE.

When transliterators hear the words *easier, faster,* or *funnier,* the suffix *er* shows an action done at a different degree. Transliterators can add the sign MORE in front of the signs EASY, FAST, or FUNNY to convey the meaning or add the signed suffix ER, which is based on the sign BEST. This should not be confused with the agent sign that represents ER in nouns.

When words end with the suffix *ility,* such as *affordability* and *accessibility,* these words can be clearly transliterated with the sign CAN inserted into the sentence along with the root word. In the sentence,

> When we look at the project, we must look at the affordability to the company

the phrase *affordability to the company* is restructured into COMPANY + CAN + AFFORD.

Transliterators need to know the parts of speech in English and how they affect transliterating. English has eight classes into which most grammarians group words according to their form changes and their position, meaning, and use in a sentence (Hodges & Whitten, 1982). The eight classes or parts of speech are listed below:

- verbs

- nouns

- pronouns

- adjectives

- adverbs

- interjections

- conjunctions

- prepositions

We will look at verbs, nouns, and pronouns in this chapter; adjectives, adverbs and interjections in Chapter 8; and conjunctions and prepositions in Chapter 9.

Verbs and Nouns

Verb. A part of speech denoting action, occurrence, or existence.

Noun. A part of speech that names a person, place, or thing.

In ASL, nouns and verbs may be related, as in the signs FOOD and EAT or CHAIR and SIT. In noun/verb combinations, the same word may be used for the noun and verb, such as TEST. In the sentences *Give me the test* and *I will test you tomorrow*, the word *test* serves as both a noun and a verb. The way certain signs are produced can change the meaning to either a verb or a noun. When adding *ing* to an English noun, it sometimes becomes a verb. For example, when the noun *parent* adds the suffix *ing*, it becomes the verb *parenting*. This requires transliterators to differentiate the verb *parenting* from the noun *parent* by adding a sign such as SKILLS to the sign PARENT.

The words *age* and *aging* are another example. *Age* is a noun that means "a period of time," and *aging* is an intransitive verb that shows the act of becoming older. *Age* is a double movement; *aging* is BECOME + OLD.

An English verb with the suffix *able* added to it becomes an adjective that denotes an action, occurrence, or thing that is capable. The sign used to demonstrate this change is CAN. Verbs with *able* added to them become adjectives. Two examples are listed below:

Eatable = something that you are able to eat = sign CAN + EAT

Debatable = something that can be debated = sign CAN + DEBATE

But there are exceptions. *Comfort* is a verb meaning "to soothe or console," or a noun that means "a state of ease." The addition of the suffix *able* changes the verb to *comfortable,* an adjective that means "providing or giving comfort." Transliterators cannot use the sign COMFORTABLE, which is an adjective, for the English word *comfort*, but instead can sign HELP, SUPPORT, or ENCOURAGE, which are also verbs.

He was a comfort to her in her old age.

That chair is comfortable.

The suffix *able* added to a noun changes the word to an adjective. The word *sizable* is an adjective that means an item is fairly large, while the word *size* is a noun that means "physical dimension or proportion." The adjective would be signed LARGE; the noun would be signed MEASUREMENT.

The suffix *ing* added to a noun sometimes creates a verb. The transliterator needs to analyze the true meaning, as in the sentences below:

I own a horse

Quit horsing around

The suffix *ment* added to a verb creates a noun and may cause a different sign to be used, as in these three examples:

govern = verb/government = noun

He will govern the group. Our government is a democracy.

settle = verb/settlement = noun

We will settle this later. They lived in a small settlement.

pay = verb/payment = noun

I will pay $10.00. My payment is in the mail.

Pluralization of Nouns

Transliterators follow the same pluralization rules found in ASL when transliterating to an English-based sign language. Pluralization is done in three different ways. The pluralization rules in ASL are as follows:

1. A double movement or repetition at the end of the noun. When a singular noun becomes a plural, there is a reduplication in the movement of the stem (Padden, 1998; Klima & Bellugi, 1979). In a sign like SISTER, the movement of the two hands coming together is the stem. In the sentence,

    We all have sisters

    transliterators use a double movement at the stem of the sign to indicate pluralization.

2. Place a number indicator before the noun (Baker & Cokely, 1980). If,

instead of *We all have sisters,* the transliterator hears,

I have two sisters

the sign TWO indicates that the sign SISTER is plural. Quantifiers in front of the noun, such as MANY or FEW, are another way transliterators indicate pluralization, and there is no reduplication necessary in the noun.

3.　Follow the noun with the sign PEOPLE or with a plural classifier (Baker & Cokely, 1890). An example is in the sentence below,

Our organization is made up of professionals.

The transliterator signs PROFESSIONAL + GROUP (the plural classifier) to show pluralization. Merely signing the word PROFESSIONAL twice can be seen as *Our organization is made up of professions.*

Modals

Modals are not one of the eight grammatical classes of English, but are characteristically used with verbs to express mood or tense. Modals cannot be used alone, but must be combined with a main verb. In ASL, modals can be used at the end of the sentence, precede the verb, or both (Humphries et al., 1994). Transliterators can stay within the rules of ASL and the grammar of English by placing the modal before the verb. The more commonly used modals are *can, could, may, might, would, must,* and *should.*

Can primarily expresses ability.

You can do that.

Could expresses possibility, doubt, or something dependent on conditions.

We could go, if your father gets home early.

May is used to indicate possibility or permission.

You may go to the movies after you clean your room.

Might is used to express a more doubtful possibility than *may.*

He might get back before Friday.

Would expresses customary action in the past.

With our last president, we would start the meetings on time.

Must expresses necessity or obligation.

You must call the agency right now.

Should is used to express likelihood or obligation.

We should arrive at the meeting 30 minutes early.

Modals do not express statements of fact, but rather they indicate actions or events that are a possibility or a necessity (Graduate School, 1998).

Pronouns

Pronoun. A part of speech that takes the position of a noun.

Pronouns in ASL are made by pointing to a person, place, or thing that is present in the area or to a specific location in the signing space that has been assigned to that person, place, or thing (Baker & Cokely, 1982). The term ASL uses to denote pronouns is *pronominalization*. In the sentences below,

Diane is my daughter. She is in the third grade.

the noun is *Diane*, and the pronoun is *she*. When a pronoun has been established, the noun is referred to as the antecedent for that particular pronoun.

Before a transliterator can use a pronoun, the noun needs to be identified and a location established in order to index it for future reference. One feature about pronouns in ASL is that nouns, not verbs, are pronomialized. When you have an English word, such as *book,* which can serve as both a noun and a verb, the sign can be indexed if it is a noun. In *Here is the test,* you can index the sign for TEST, but in *I will test you next week*, you cannot index the verb.

The Word *who*

The English word *who* serves as a question marker and a relative pronoun. In ASL, the sign WHO is used as a question marker or as a grammatical signal to a rhetorical question (Baker & Cokely, 1980). In English when *who* is used in a question such as *Who left the class?* then the sign WHO would be used by the transliterator. But when the English word *who* is used as a relative pronoun, then pronominalization occurs. An example is,

The girl who came here yesterday.

The pronoun is *girl,* and *who* refers back to the antecedent, *girl.* The English word *who* can be represented by the ASL pronoun HE, SHE, or IT.

Sometimes transliterators use the sign SELF when the word *who* is not referring back to the antecedent but representing an attribute of the subject. Below is a comparison of the three uses of *who:*

That brown haired woman, who is she? (sign WHO)

That woman, who is my son's teacher, got an award last week. (index)

I set my best friend up with my cousin, who is smart and beautiful. (sign SELF)

The Word *it*

It is a pronoun in English that represents the third person or references the last thing mentioned. The interesting part about the word *it* is that the transliterator sometimes forgets what *it* represents. After establishing a noun, the transliterator then references the noun by using pronominalization as it is used in ASL. When hearing the word *it*, the transliterator can sign the noun a second time in order to establish what *it* represents. But the word *it* can be problematic, as seen in the following sentences:

First, a few things about my company. We were started in 1969. It is a non-profit organization for children.

The pronoun *it* and the antecedent *company* are separated by a sentence. The transliterator signs COMPANY for *company*. When the English word *it* comes up later, the transliterator signs COMPANY again and references an area with an index. From then on, the pronominalization of IT represents the company.

Now perhaps the transliterator encounters the sentence below:

Although we are becoming older, we should be enjoying it.

The transliterator represents *it* with the verb clause *becoming older*. In this example, the signs used for *becoming older* are repeated but not pronomialized.

SUMMARY

Transliterators strive to follow English word order while at the same time maintaining the meaning behind the words. If transliterators only follow surface meaning, the overall meaning may be lost.

English has eight grammatical classes into which words are grouped according to their meanings and uses in a sentence. The grammatical placement of a word in English will dictate how transliterators convey that word. A word in English may be a verb or a noun, but the way ASL depicts verbs and nouns is different. Transliterators need to make adjustments according to the meaning and grammatical placement of the English text.

Nouns pluralized in English can be pluralized three ways: a double movement at the end of the noun; a number indicator signed before the noun; or a sign added to the noun that denotes pluralization, such as PEOPLE or GROUP.

Pronouns are referred to as pronominalization in ASL. Before a pronoun can be used, a noun needs to be identified and a location established. Pronouns in English that may cause transliterators difficulty are *who* and *it*. One can pronominalize a noun, but not a verb.

Modals, such as *can, could, may, might, would, must,* and *should,* are used with verbs in order to express mood or tense. They do not express a statement of fact, but indicate an event that is a possibility or a necessity.

ACTIVITIES

Activity 7-1

Look at the sentence pairs. Decide how the common word would be transliterated

Example: I am a parent. I am taking parenting classes.

I am a parent. I take parent skill classes.

1. I am going to work now. How can we work out our problems?

2. My father runs the company. I have a run in my nylons.

3. My house is near the store. Where are the records housed?

4. The poll shows Clarke ahead. We start the polling this week.

5. I belong to the human race. I won the race.

6. The book is on the table. I move to table the motion.

7. I bought a new truck. You want to truck the sofa across town?

8. Take the 201A Bus. Bus your own dishes.

9. I like jazz music. Let's jazz this place up.

10. Here is your test. Let me test that recipe.

11. What field are you in? I will field that question.

Activity 7-2

The following story will help you practice transliterating based on the words *it* and *who*. You may either have one person read the story to you, or you may read the story and do consecutive transliterating.

I am here today to tell you that unless the price of gas goes down there will be problems. If we feel we are not being treated fairly, we will complain. <u>Who</u> among us has not felt the strain of paying higher prices? But <u>who</u> has complained? In an economy where the price of gas is allowed to run rampant, <u>it</u> is the poor and middle class <u>who</u> suffer the most. <u>It</u> must not be able to go on. I say, unless we set up new federal programs to reverse this trend, we will continue to see higher gas prices.

This must stop, and <u>it</u> must stop now. Someone must step forward to take the lead. <u>Who</u> can this be? <u>Who</u> will be willing to come forward? <u>It</u> is imperative to have a leader. Will <u>it</u> be the mayor only <u>who</u> is involved in city issues? Or will <u>it</u> be the governor <u>who</u> regulates state law? We don't know <u>who</u> <u>it</u> will be, but no matter <u>who</u> steps forward, <u>it</u> must be a person <u>who</u> possesses the skills needed to address the issues. And no matter <u>who</u> steps forward, <u>it</u> is up to us to ask the questions and to try to solve the problems. We must take care of <u>it</u>, now and forever.

■■ CHAPTER 8

Adjectives, Adverbs, and Interjections

ADJECTIVES

Adjective. A part of speech that modifies a noun.

Adjectives are modifiers that limit, describe, or qualify nouns. Examples are *beautiful, tall, courteous, deep, incomplete,* and *low.* This type of adjective usually does not cause transliterators any problems. But many adjectives do not start out as adjectives. When suffixes such as *al, able, ant, ative, ic, ish, less, ous,* or *y* are added to certain verbs or nouns, adjectives are formed. For example, the word *accept* is a verb. When the suffix *able* is added, the word becomes *acceptable,* an adjective. Transliterators make this clear in translations by signing CAN with the verb ACCEPT to convey the meaning *acceptable.*

If the English noun *effort* has the suffix *less* added, the word becomes the adjective *effortless.* Transliterators can sign WITHOUT along with the sign EFFORT.

When the suffix *ful* is added to the verb *use,* the verb becomes the adjective *useful.* But with this adjective, transliterators cannot use the same root sign, but must use another sign. For example, in the sentence,

> That is a useful book

transliterators cannot sign USE + FULL but might instead sign HELP + MUCH or just GOOD. When the suffix *y* is added to the noun *sleep,* it becomes the adjective *sleepy.* Transliterators only need to add a double movement to the sign SLEEP to show the adjective SLEEPY. Transliterators must be aware of when verbs and nouns become adjectives and adjust their output accordingly.

ADVERBS

Adverb. A part of speech regularly used to describe or limit a verb.

Adverbs modify a verb, an adjective, or another adverb. Adverbs can be identified by answering one of the following questions:

Where? *I have my money <u>here</u>.*

When? *Water the plants <u>daily</u>.*

How? *The girls run <u>fast.</u>*

To what extent? *The campers traveled <u>farther</u> that day.*

Verbs can be modified in ASL through the *temporal aspect,* which refers to certain repeated movements made to a verb to show how long an action lasts or how often the action occurs (Baker & Cokely, 1982). Transliterators often must incorporate the temporal aspect into their translations. In the statement below,

I frequently go to that restaurant

the transliterator would modify the sign TO GO to show the concept of "frequently." This is done by signing the verb TO GO with repeated small (non-tense) straight-line movements (Baker & Cokely, 1980).

Verbs that indicate that something has been happening for a long time have a slow elliptical movement added (Baker & Cokely, 1980). This occurs in a sentence such as,

The baby cried forever.

The sign CRIED has an elliptical movement added to show that the crying occurred over a long period of time.

To indicate the concept of prolonged activity, the movement of the verb is a straight line followed by an arc-like movement back to the initiating point of the verb (Baker & Cokely, 1980). In the sentence,

I kept looking at the picture, over and over

the verb TO LOOK would be presented with this arc-like movement before continuing with the rest of the sentence.

Transliterators still use the English adverbs *frequently, forever,* and *over and over* during the task of transliterating, and they may not be able to make the movements of the temporal aspect as big or as long as interpreters do. The English structure is not changed by the use of the temporal aspect, but the verb is clarified through its use.

The Word *now*

The English word *now* is an adverb, but it can also serve as a discourse marker and time indicator. As a discourse marker, the word *now* shows that there is a topic shift in the discourse. This is demonstrated by the sentence,

Now, let's look at the impact cars have on the environment.

The word *now* indicates that the topic that was being discussed before is finished and the speaker will be moving on to a new topic.

In ASL, the sign NOW is a time indicator that refers to something occurring in the present. In the English sentence

Now we can break for lunch

the time indicator NOW would be appropriate. However, the transliterator may encounter the English word *now* and decide the word is being used as a shift in topic rather than a temporal marker. If the English word *now* is being used to indicate a shift in topic, then the transliterator can use signs such as ANYWAY or NEXT or simply delete it. In the example below:

> First we must look at pollution's effect on wildlife. Now what would be one effect?

the word *now* is not a time indicator but rather a discourse marker. In this case, the transliterator would eliminate the word *now* and begin transliterating at the word *what*.

In this next example,

> ... and then we got married. Now 10 years, later we ...

now indicates a shift in topic, not a temporal marker, as the *now* in the sentence may mean 15 years ago, so ANYWAY is used.

INTERJECTIONS

> **Interjection.** A part of speech used for simple exclamations.

Interjections are words such as *oh, ouch, wow,* or *whew.* Transliterators do not have to take into account any special consideration for these words, which can be presented as either a sign or a fingerspelled word.

SUMMARY

Adjectives are modifiers that limit, describe, or qualify nouns. Various signed English systems have separate signs for suffixes. Transliterators do not sign the suffixes added to certain verbs or nouns to form adjectives. However, since suffixes may change the meaning of the root word, transliterators need to know how the root word changes and sign them accordingly. Various signs can be used to convey the meaning of the message, which may or may not retain the original root word.

Adverbs are used to modify a verb, an adjective, or another adverb. In ASL, verbs are modified by using the temporal aspect of the sign. The temporal aspect is certain repeated movements done to the verb and may be repeated small straight-line movements to show the concept of "frequently," an elliptical movement to show the concept of "over a long period of time," or a straight-line repeated movement to show the concept of prolonged activity.

Interjections are used for simple exclamations. Transliterators should handle them the same way an interpreter does.

ACTIVITIES

Activity 8-1

In this activity, the word *now* is used. Decide if *now* is being used as a discourse marker, adverb, or time indicator. Transliterate the text.

Now, have you ever run into the problem of misplacing something, like your keys, and then not been able to find them? I sense we have all shared this experience every now and then. I remember one time when this happened to me. I was sent a list of names, and I decided to put the list in a safe place, so I could easily find it later. Well, later became now, and I needed that list.

So I began searching for the list in some possible places, but with no luck. Now I was upset. I knew I had put it in a safe place, but why was it so difficult to find now? So I did something I suspect we all do from time to time, I now began to search through the same places I had just finished going through. Now, don't you think that was clever. You see, if I couldn't find the list, I would have to admit I lost it and then ask for another one.

Now I didn't plan to lose the list and I didn't want to admit I had lost it. But now I can tell you, I found the list, where I thought I left it, in my desk, where I now keep all important papers.

Activity 8-2

In this exercise, look at how suffixes change parts of speech depending on the word position in the sentence. Look through the text to familiarize yourself with it, and circle words that have suffixes. Transliterate the text.

Summer is getting closer. The days are getting longer, and the sun is moving higher across the sky. There are lots of sunny, playful days ahead. But over the years, this has been counterproductive for your skin.

Hidden in all that sunshine is something your eye is incapable of seeing. It's a part of the sun's ultraviolet rays, called UVB. It is so damaging that most living things had to develop some kind of protective cover to screen it out. Your skin protects you by absorbing UVB.

Just as in other animals, human skin has some melanin. This is a dark pigmentation that is a good absorber of UVB. Our skin colors vary widely, so some of us are more sensitive to sun than others. Skin with less pigment is more sensitive to the sun's harmful rays.

You might already know about sunburn. You go to the beach or out for a long, idyllic hike early in the summer. That is when your skin takes a big dose of sun. Later that night, you realize your skin is burned badly–it feels hot and probably hurts. In a few days, the burn will heal and your skin will feel well again.

You might also know about suntan. That's what happens to many of us when we are exposed to the sun a little at a time. Tanning is the skin's way of being protective by making more melanin. A suntan looks nice, but by the time you get one, the deeper layers of skin have been damaged. Over time, the skin's elastic fibers gradually lose the stretchiness that keeps your skin tight and smooth.

Though it may happen very gradually, the skin tends to get leathery and wrinkled. Years of exposure to UVB makes you susceptible to skin cancer. Fortunately, we can protect our skin from UVB. One good way is to pick the right time of day to be outside. That way we can use the earth's atmosphere to screen out UVB more completely.

■■ CHAPTER 9

Conjunctions and Prepositions

CONJUNCTIONS

Conjunction. A part of speech used to connect and relate words, phrases, clauses, or sentences

In English there are two types of conjunctions: coordinating and subordinating. First, we will look at coordinating conjunctions.

Coordinating Conjunctions

Coordinating conjunctions are used to connect phrases that are of equal and independent grammatical rank, or two main clauses that can each stand alone. Examples of coordinating conjunctions include *and, but, or, nor, for, so,* and *yet.* An example of the coordinating conjunction *and* is in the sentence below:

I like to read, and my hobby is collecting stamps.

You could also state,

I like to read. My hobby is collecting stamps.

Each phrase in the first example can stand alone. Transliterators can sign AND or PLUS. At times, the glossed term for the sign is not the appropriate sign to use for the English gloss coordinating conjunction. In the sentence,

I want to go to the store and then rent a movie

the *and* is not needed. What is critical is the concept of *then.* Transliterators can sign THEN after STORE and before RENT. An example of the coordinating conjunction *or* is in the following sentence:

Eric will study history or he will study English.

Transliterators can sign EITHER or fingerspell the word O-R. If the transliterator sets up the number 2 on the nondominant hand and shows these as *either,* then *history* can be referenced on the index finger, and *English* can be referenced on the middle finger. Another example of the coordinating conjunction *or* is,

We can either go to dinner and then a movie, or go to the movie first.

Transliterators can use space in this sentence to enhance clarity. By listing the dinner and movie on one side and the idea of the movie first on the other side, there is a clear comparison. Another way is to fingerspell O-R while moving from one side to another. In the sentence,

> I want neither to go to the movies, nor to go out at all

the coordinating conjunction is *nor*. Because coordinating clauses can stand alone, transliterators can make two statements. By repeating DON'T-WANT for *nor* in the second statement, it can be restructured to I + DON'T-WANT + GO-OUT and still maintain English word order.

Subordinating Conjunctions

Subordinating conjunctions mark a dependent clause that is connected with a main clause. Unlike the two main clauses connected by a coordinating conjunction, a subordinating clause cannot stand alone and is dependent on the other clause. Subordinating conjunctions are *after, although, as, because, as if, before, if, since, unless, until, when*, and *while*.

In ASL, subordinating conjunctions are conditional sentences, or if/then sentences. The conditional sentence in ASL has two parts. One part states a condition—this is the "if" clause—and one part states what will happen if that condition is or is not met—this is the "then" clause. An example of a conditional sentence is,

> If I get the job, then I will buy a new car.

In ASL, the condition portion is generally signed first. When transliterators hear these subordinating conjunctions, they should wait to see if the sentence coming up is a conditional sentence. By understanding the subordinating conjunction in English, they are able to transliterate the appropriate meaning.

> If a company advertises, then it will sell more products.

In this sentence, transliterators use appropriate facial and body markers of the conditional sentence. The markers for the condition "if" include raised eyebrows, the head tilted in one direction, and the body slightly inclined. There is a pause between the "if" clause and the "then" clause of the sentence. For the "then" clause, the appropriate non-manual markers are a slight pause and a grammatical change that is appropriate to the segment. But transliterating from English to an English-based sign language is not always simply changing an English conjunction to an ASL if/then sentence. The previous example can also be restated as,

> The company that advertises sells more products.

This sentence is still a conditional sentence, but there are no clear if/then markers. The sentence is still handled as a conditional sentence with appropriate non-manual markers. The next two sentences,

If a manager pays well, then they will have a more productive staff

Managers who pay well have a more productive staff

have the same meaning. With each sentence, the subordinating clause is dependent on the main clause. There is an action and then a reaction, and transliterators
would sign both examples as conditional sentences. The sentence below,

I will look for work in July if I graduate in June

is a conditional sentence, but it is not presented in the same order as it would be
in ASL. Transliterators would restructure the sentence by putting the conditional,
if I graduate in June, first, followed by what will happen, *I will look for work in
July*. Another option is to simply use the appropriate non-manual markers, head
tilted and body slightly inclined, to show the conditional in the second part of
the sentence.

PREPOSITIONS

> **Preposition.** A part of speech that links and relates a word to some
> other word in the sentence.

In English, prepositions are used to link a word to another word. In ASL, locatives
function as prepositions. "*Locatives* are ways of describing the spatial relationship between two or more people, places, or things" (Baker & Cokely, 1982).
Prepositions can cause problems when interpreters are learning to transliterate
because ASL generally does not use a separate sign to describe spatial relationship, but rather uses signing space. In the task of transliterating, prepositions
need to be more explicitly signed. There are several separate locative signs in
ASL, which include IN, ON, UNDER, NEAR, and BETWEEN (Baker & Cokely, 1982).

Some prepositions in English are *at, before, behind, by, in, of, on, over, into, to*,
and *with*. Many of these prepositions can have more than one meaning as they
fall into more than one part of speech. When following English structure, transliterators must be aware of the specific meaning of the preposition to sign the
preposition appropriately. Prepositions should be thought of as connecting
words. An example of a preposition in an English sentence is found below:

These paintings should be hung in the hall.

The preposition *in* connects and relates the word *hall*, the object of the preposition, to the word *hung,* the verb. Perhaps because prepositions are often small
words and are not distinct and separate items in ASL, transliterators tend to
ignore them. Prepositions, however, are not deleted by interpreters, but rather
incorporated into ASL using classifiers, directional verbs, or indexing. If a transliterator deletes prepositions, the meaning of the sentence can be lost or become
ambiguous. Consider the following text:

We are a country of the people, by the people, and for the people.

Without the prepositions the sentence reads as

> We are a country, the people, the people, and the people.

The following paragraphs provide more detailed explanations of the prepositions *to, of,* and *by.*

The Word *to*

The word *to* in ASL is used for direction or to show how something is given or done to a specific person. TO is signed when the English word *toward* can be substituted for the word *to*. The English word *to* would not be signed by the transliterator when it acts as an infinitive verb, such as in the following two examples:

> The City School Board tries to focus on parent concerns.

> The company is doing its best to give its employees information.

In the following example, *to* serves as an infinitive verb and a preposition:

> I want to talk to Sally.

The first *to* is an infinitive verb and is incorporated into the sign TALK. The second *to* is a preposition and can be signed WITH. The English word *to* has 27 definitions in the dictionary (Morris, 1980). Below are some definitions of the word *to* along with corresponding signs:

Definition	Example	Sign
In the direction of	I'm going to Scotland.	TO
In contact with	Apply lotion to the skin.	ON
Through and including	I worked to the end.	UNTIL
As an addition	Dance to the music.	WITH
With regard to	It's the secret to my success.	FOR

The Word *of*

The English word *of* has 19 definitions in the dictionary (Morris, 1980). Below are some definitions of the word *of* along with corresponding signs:

Definition	Example	Sign
Show distance	a mile east of here	FROM
Show	a man of your status	WITH
Direct toward	a love of horses	FOR
Reference something	think highly of his idea	ABOUT
Set aside	a day of rest	FOR

There will be instances when the word *of* can be deleted without losing any meaning of the message. *Of* does not have to be included when used as an identifying label in phrases such as

> patch of flowers

> group of people

> basket of groceries

> herd of cattle

The Word *by*

The English preposition *by* has 13 definitions (Morris, 1980) and can be transliterated in a variety of ways. Below are some definitions of the word *by* along with the corresponding signs:

Definition	Example	Sign
To be next to something	the car by the house	NEAR
Up to and beyond	he drove by the school	PAST
A time period	sleeping by day	DURING
To be not later than	meet you by 5:00 p.m.	BEFORE
In the presence of	I swear by God	IN FRONT OF

With just these few examples of *to, of,* and *by,* you can see that prepositions are a critical part of meaning. To do the task of transliterating well, the transliterator looks to understand the relationship between objects and then decide which sign will be best, based on English, to convey the meaning to the consumer.

SUMMARY

In English, conjunctions are used to connect and relate words, phrases, clauses, or sentences. Conjunctions can be either coordinating or subordinating. Coordinating conjunctions connect words and phrases of equal grammatical rank. Subordinating conjunctions mark a dependent clause and connect it with a main clause. They work the same way as a conditional sentence does in ASL.

Transliterators can use the non-manual markers of a conditional sentence in sentences with subordinating conjunctions.

Prepositions are a part of speech that link and relate a word to a noun in the sentence. In ASL, prepositions are regularly incorporated by interpreters using classifiers and are referred to as "locatives." When following an English-based sentence structure, transliterators need to incorporate prepositions overtly back into the sentence.

Prepositions that are of interest are *to, of,* and *by.* Transliterators should look for the English concept meant by these prepositions and make the appropriate sign choice in the English-based sign language.

ACTIVITIES

Activity 9-1

Transliterate the following sentences. Identify whether the sentence contains a coordinating or subordinating conjunction. Underline each clause and circle the word connecting the clauses.

Example:

After I work for 2 years, then I will take a European vacation.

After I work for 2 years, (*then*) *I will take a European vacation.*

1. Although I have a degree, I can't find the job I want.

2. Because I have children in school, I still take summers off.

3. Before I go out tonight, I must finish my work.

4. If I graduate in June, then I will look for work in July.

5. Since I learned to dance, I go out more often.

6. Unless you clean your room, you can't go out tonight.

7. When you have finished your dinner, you can have dessert.

8. I like neither cake nor pie.

9. While I am out shopping, can I pick anything up for you?

10. I would like to see a movie, but I also want to go shopping.

11. My husband wants to buy a truck, but I want to buy a car.

12. The temperature was not only below zero, but the wind was blowing.

13. I want to visit France, Germany, and Great Britain this summer.

14. Should I go abroad or stay home?

15. I got married last year, so my taxes went down.

Activity 9-2

Circle all the prepositions in the text, decide their meanings, and write what sign, if any, you will use. Practice transliterating.

One spring day, John decided to take a walk through the woods. John put his old hat made of straw on his head, went out of his house, and walked to the woods. When he had walked for a long time, he sat down on a big rock to rest by a tree. He took off his hat and laid it on the grass beside him.

Up jumped his hat. Then up jumped John. John chased his hat but he couldn't catch it. The hat jumped over a log. John jumped over the log and chased his hat down the path. The hat jumped by Farmer Bob's house. John ran by Farmer Bob's house. The hat jumped through a patch of flowers. John jumped through the patch of flowers and followed his hat to a stream.

The hat jumped across the stream on three flat rocks. John ran to the stream and jumped on the first two flat rocks, but missed the last one. SPLASH! John fell into the stream and under the water. John pulled himself out of the stream and saw his hat disappear into a hollow log. He ran around to the other end of the log and waited.

Out came the hat. The hat jumped right into John's hands. John looked under his hat. He laughed. "I'm sorry, frog," he said. "You can't have my hat. You will have to find one of your own." And the fat green frog hopped away down the road.

■■ CHAPTER 10

Passive and Active Voice

THE ATTRIBUTES OF VOICE

In every language, discourse is presented in a variety of ways. How one's culture expresses an idea may not be the way it is presented in another culture. For example, Shelley Lawrence (1995) found features in ASL that made ASL three-dimensional. These features, referred to as "ASL expansion," are not present in English. English also contains features not found, or not as prevalent, in ASL. One example is a feature called "voice," which can be either active or passive. The technical definition of "voice" is:

> The form of a transitive verb that indicates whether or not the subject performs the action denoted by the verb. A verb with a direct object is in the active voice. When the direct object is converted into a subject, the verb is in the passive voice.

(Hodges & Whitten, 1982, p. 557)

PASSIVE AND ACTIVE VOICE

Most sentences in ASL are in the active voice. The basic form of an active voice sentence is a subject, a verb, and a direct object, such as

The boy kicked the ball.

The *boy* is the subject, *kicked* is the verb, and the direct object is the *ball*. The subject, *boy*, does the action, which in this case is *kicked*.

This same sentence can be expressed in the passive voice in English by restructuring the sentence. The basic form of a passive sentence is an object, a form of "to be," a verb, the word *by*, and finally the subject. Below is the same sentence in passive voice:

The ball was kicked by the boy.

In the above sentence, the object is the *ball*, the form of "to be" is *was*, and the verb is still *kicked*. By adding the word *by* followed by the subject, which is still the *boy*, you have a passive sentence. Both the active and the passive sentences still have the same meaning. A simple comparison of the two types of sentences is found below.

Active Voice

The boy	kicked	the ball.
subject	*verb*	*object*

Passive Voice

The ball	was	kicked	by	the boy.
Object	*"to be"*	*verb*	*"by"*	*subject*

The challenge for transliterators is that ASL rarely uses the passive voice. If the passive sentence is signed in exact English word order, the signed sentence would look like BALL + KICK + BOY. Since passive and active sentences have the same meaning and only the form has changed, the active voice sentence *The boy kicked the ball* is considered a restructuring of the sentence. With the restructured sentence now in active voice, the mouthing would follow the new form.

Another example of passive voice is taken from the computer field in the following sentence,

Highs were dominated by lows.

If the transliterator follows the English word order and signs HIGH + CONTROL + LOW, ignoring the preposition *by*, the meaning is opposite of the true meaning of the English sentence. In order to retain the intended meaning, the sentence must be changed into active voice:

The lows dominated the highs.

Some transliterators would transliterate this sentence in the passive voice and add the fingerspelled word B-Y. However, this would not be as clear as transliterating into an active voice, especially if the word *lows* is also fingerspelled.

Not all passive sentences contain the "by" phrase. When the "by" phrase is eliminated, the performer of the action is either unknown or is not the focus of attention. This can be seen in the following two passive voice sentences:

The jewelry was stolen by burglars.

The jewelry was stolen.

Both sentences are in the passive voice. In the first sentence, the jewelry is stolen by unnamed burglars as the subject. In the second sentence, there is no subject mentioned. Both sentences have similar meanings, but not the same form.

The challenge of voice occurs if there is not enough processing time for the transliterator to recognize that a sentence is in passive voice in order to restructure the sentence into an active sentence. One way to recognize passive/active voice is to listen for a noun followed by a "to be" verb, like *The car was....* When this occurs, the transliterator should wait. If the next word is an adjective that describes the noun—*The car was green*—the "to be" verb is acting as a copula. A copula is a verb that identifies a predicate that expresses a characteristic or attribute of the subject. This is demonstrated in the following active sentences:

> The boy is happy.

> The carpet is gray.

In the above examples, transliterators can use the sign SELF in place of the copula. But if the "to be" verb is followed by another verb, the sentence is passive. This is demonstrated in the following sentences:

> The car was washed by my son.

> The boy is taught to ski.

> The carpet will be installed by the Sunset Co.

When the word following the form of "to be" is a verb, then it is an auxiliary verb, and the transliterator should wait for the subject of the verb in order to change the passive sentence into an active sentence. The following are examples of passive and active sentences with the grammatical structure broken down.

Passive Voice

John	was chosen	by	Sue.
object	*"to be" verb*	*by*	*subject*

Active Voice

Sue	chose	John.
subject	*verb*	*object*

In the next examples, the subject is not mentioned.

Passive Voice

A	new	secretary	will be	hired.
article	*adjective*	*object*	*"to be"*	*verb*

Active Voice

The boss	will hire	a	new	secretary.
subject	*verb phrase*	*article*	*adjective*	*object*

The subject, who will hire the secretary, is eliminated in the passive sentence and may not be as important as the hiring itself. If the passive sentence were signed exactly as spoken, it would appear as if the secretary was doing the hiring.

Passive Voice

I	dislike	being	ignored.
object	*verb*	*"to be"*	*verb*

The first verb, *dislike*, is related to the object, *I*; the second verb, *ignored,* is related to the subject, which is not mentioned. It is not known whether the person dislikes being ignored by other people in general, by family members, or by students in a classroom. Although the subject in this sentence is unknown, the transliterator can gain this information through context and then incorporate the subject into the sentence. Transliterators can sign the above sentence in two sentences in order to make the passive voice an active voice sentence.

Active Voice

PEOPLE	*IGNORE*	*ME*	/	*ME*	*NOT-LIKE*
subject	*verb*	*object*	/	*subject*	*verb*

Another way to handle passive sentences is to change the verb. Transliterators can sign the following sentence by changing the verb *given* to the verb *received*.

Passive Voice

The contract	was	given	to	Smith Co.
object	*"to be"*	*verb*	*preposition*	*object*

Active Voice

Smith Co.	received	the contract.
object	*verb*	*subject*

In the next example, the verb *taught* is changed to the verb *learned*.

Passive Voice

The student	was	taught	fractions.
object	*"to be"*	*verb*	*indirect object*

Active Voice

The student   learned   fractions.

subject   *verb*   *object*

The meaning is the same for both examples, and the passive sentence becomes active.

Some passive sentences do not have to be changed to an active sentence, as it is sometimes possible to sign a passive sentence and still make sense in the signed language. The following sentences are examples.

The flowers were picked yesterday.

FLOWERS + FINISH + PICK + YESTERDAY

The wine was produced in California.

WINE + MADE + INDEX/CALIFORNIA

The house was painted yesterday.

HOUSE + FINISH + PAINT + YESTERDAY

In these sentences, the word *by* and the subject are missing, and the transliterator would sign the sentences as presented. None of the examples above show who did the action, but in these sentences, the person who picked the flowers, produced the wine, or painted the house brings no additional meaning to the sentence.

SUMMARY

Sentences in English are presented in either active voice or passive voice, but sentences in ASL are presented more often in active voice. To ensure that the meaning is conveyed accurately, the transliterator should wait, identify the voice, and change a passive sentence into an active sentence if necessary.

A typical active voice sentence is made up of a subject, a transitive verb, and a direct object. A typical passive voice sentence is made up of an object, a "to be" verb, an auxiliary verb, the word *by*, and a subject.

Not all passive sentences are handled in the same way. Some passive sentences can be signed in the same order as the spoken English, while others need to be completely restructured. Some passive sentences include the subject and some do not. In some situations, all a transliterator needs to do is change the verb.

Tense does not affect passive sentences, which can be presented in past, present, or future tense. The position of the subject and object in the spoken English sentence is critical. Transliterators using a short processing time will need to extend that time to identify whether a sentence is passive or active. If the transliterator hears a noun followed by a form of "to be," they should wait. If the next word is an adjective, the "to be" is a copula and identifies a characteristic or attribute of the subject. The sentence can be signed as presented with the sign SELF used in place of the copula. However, if the next word is a verb, then the sentence is passive and the transliterator waits to hear the whole sentence in order to decide whether to restructure it.

ACTIVITIES

Exercise 10-1

Change the passive sentences into active sentences. Sentences 1-5 contain an explicit subject. Sentences 6-13 do not contain an explicit subject.

Example:

Pennies are thrown into the fountain by tourists.

Tourists throw pennies into the fountain.

1. Bob was given $5.00 by Sam.

2. The theory of relativity was invented by Einstein.

3. My entire paper was read by the professor in class.

4. I feel I am not being understood by my family.

5. The professor wants to be well liked by his students.

6. I don't like it when my friend is criticized.

7. The president was assassinated.

8. I feel loved.

9. The streets will be repaved.

10. The house was built in 1924.

11. At the end of the play, the actors were greeted with a loud burst of applause.

12. People need to be fed.

13. The student will be given lunch.

Exercise 10-2

First identify all the passive sentences in the story. Change them into active sentences. Practice transliterating.

Tom had been bad in school, so he was assigned extra homework by the teacher. Tom was already behind on many of the assignments because he was the type of boy who preferred to complain about work rather than do it. This time, his teacher decided not to baby him. Tom would do his work.

You see, Tom was a born complainer. He frequently was not attentive to what the teacher was saying. Later, he would complain he did not understand what was said. It was not that Tom was a bad boy, but rather that he sought every opportunity to escape from doing work. He would often act like a clown, and the other students were amused. But this was not appreciated by the teacher.

This time, the teacher hoped that Tom could not bear the pressure she was about to deliver. In a stern voice she told Tom he would have to stay after school that day to finish his work. And if he did not do his work, he would not be able to participate in after-school sports.

Tom was furious when he realized what was happening. He was being forced to do his work. He was forced to not play sports. He had a feeling the teacher wasn't kidding this time. Tom decided he had better get busy and finish his work. He knew that excuses would no longer be accepted. He knew the teacher didn't believe what he said. She would now only react to what he did or did not do. He was stuck. He now would have to do the schoolwork that was assigned to him.

■■ CHAPTER 11

Putting It All Together

GETTING STARTED

When students finish a class or a book, there is sometimes the feeling of, "I'm done, I've learned everything." Well the fact is, this is just the beginning. All interpreters, no matter what skill they want to learn, are always in the state of "becoming." And this becoming means they are always striving and never arriving (Kelly, 1998). So, as interpreters wanting to learn the task of transliterating, we take on the process of life-long learning. This book has helped you build a foundation of knowledge and skills, but you will need to continue working on your skills. You should recognize that there are four different levels of learning as defined by O'Connor & Seymour (1990):

Unconscious incompetence

Conscious incompetence

Conscious competence

Unconscious competence

As transliterators, we all have areas in which we are not as proficient as we could be. We can get the message out while transliterating, but do not realize where the message could be clearer. This level is *unconscious incompetence*. As we begin to work on skill development, as we open ourselves up to improvement, either through self-critiquing or mentorship, we become aware of our lack of proficiency. This moves us to the next level, *conscious incompetence*.

Conscious incompetence is when we become aware of what we need to learn. While working on developing a new skill, many errors are made and the temptation is strong to revert to the old way of doing things. In fact, we may sometimes feel like we were better off before we knew what needed fixing. This stage is uncomfortable and can be frustrating, but it is during this stage that we learn the most.

The next level, *conscious competence*, is the state in which the correct way to do a task has been learned, but the skill being worked on still requires a great deal of effort and concentration to perform correctly. The skill has been learned, but not mastered. While performing our new skills, we begin to notice improvement.

Eventually, we arrive at the last stage of learning, *unconscious competence*.

Unconscious competence is gained after we have worked at a skill long enough for it to become automatic. Yet, as one new competence is gained, another incompetence is waiting to be discovered, and the cycle begins again. There is no set time for how long it takes a person to move through the four stages of learning. For some people and some skills, it takes only an awareness of the incompetence and a short time to move through all four stages, while at other times, it may take weeks or months to move through the four levels of learning.

STRATEGIES TO IMPROVE YOUR TRANSLITERATING

Along with the four levels of learning, there is a two-part ongoing process involved when working on improving skills. They are *evaluation* and *development* (Gordon, 1999).

Evaluation refers to the assessment of your performance. This is when you review any challenges or difficulties you may have had while transliterating. Perhaps a consumer has pointed out areas that need improvement, or maybe you have sometimes sensed you were not getting the message across clearly. This would be a good time to look at old videotapes of yourself and reflect on how you perceive yourself doing the task of transliterating up to this point.

Development looks at your future performance. The focus here is to explore not only what needs to be worked on, but also how to get there. To do this, transliterators self-assess their work, or work with another transliterator in a mentorship or partnership. Whatever choice the transliterator makes regarding future development, the first step in development is goal setting.

Goal Setting

In Lewis Carroll's book, "Alice in Wonderland" (1960), Alice asks the Cheshire Cat, "Would you tell me, please, which way I ought to go from here?" The cat replies, "That depends a good deal on where you want to get to." "I don't much care where..." says Alice. "Then it doesn't matter which way you go," says the cat.

Many times transliterators approach skill development the same way. When asked what they want to work on, they say "everything" or "I just want to get better." Yet, to get to the end of a journey, you need to know where you are going.

Bill Isham (1983) wrote an article that discussed self-directed growth for interpreters. The areas Isham looked at were goal setting, time frames, written records, feedback, and guidance. In order to set goals, you need to identify the problems. You may be aware of these problems through self-diagnosis, or from working with a mentor or a teacher in an Interpreting Preparation Program. Once you have identified the problems and set your goals, you can move on to the next step.

Goal Specificity

When identifying the problem you want to work on, be specific (Clark, 1995). "I can't transliterate" is not as specific as, "I have problems with passive sentences." "I am weak at fingerspelling" is not as constructive as "I have sloppy articulation when I fingerspell." The more specific you are about the area you want to improve, the better. Being specific will allow you to identify improvements and know when to move on to other areas. This leads us to the next step.

Prioritizing Goals

Once you have identified your problem areas, decide which ones you want to focus on first (Isham, 1983). You cannot fix everything at once. If you have five weak areas identified, pick the top two. When you feel you have improved in those areas, you move on to another area. But mentally prioritizing your goals is not enough.

Write It Down

It is easy to assume that you will work on a skill once it has been identified, but if you write it down, you will be more committed. Place your written goals in an area where you will see them often: on your mirror in the bathroom, on the refrigerator, or in your day-planner. Otherwise, you may forget about them in a week or two. Once you have your goals written down, then you need to begin working on them.

Practice

Practicing does not mean simply doing more transliterating. You need to start thinking about what you are doing as you are transliterating. Take the time to reflect on the work you do and how it can be improved. Once a concept is figured out in your head, it is easier to sign. Practice transliterating a difficult text that is above your level of comfort. Also, practice a text more than once. It is not cheating because you "know what is coming." Practicing until you get it right will help you gain confidence as well as competence.

Working with a Mentor

Mentoring does not have to be a formal situation, nor do you need an interpreter who has been in the field 25 years. If you are graduating from an Interpreting Preparation Program, an interpreter with 3 to 5 years of experience in the field can "mentor you up." You might consider someone that transliterates where you work. If you are in a college system, seek out someone with the skills you would like to emulate and ask to be partnered with that person in a mentorship capacity.

In a team situation, your team transliterator can give you feedback or just be available to answer questions. Both partners benefit during this process. Be specific in letting the mentor partner know what you expect from the mentoring relationship.

A Deaf mentor is also a possibility. Ask a Deaf individual whom you know that uses transliterators to work with you. Perhaps this person would be willing to help you in exchange for transliterating services.

Once a mentor has agreed to work with you, decide together how long the mentorship will last. There is nothing quite as uncomfortable as wanting to get out of a mentoring relationship, but not wanting to be the first person to say it. If you agree from the start that you will meet once a week for four weeks, or for a semester class, or until the mid-term, then at the end of the specified time, there can be a mutual agreement to stop. If at this point you want to continue with your mentor, then you can agree on another specific amount of time or arrange to come back later for another mentorship.

The issue of payment can be handled many ways. If you are working with someone who is already being paid for interpreting, such as in a school district or college setting, they may agree to work with you during working hours and there would be no need for payment. Deaf individuals may agree to mentor you in exchange for transliterating services. To show your appreciation to your mentor, you may want to give them a gift certificate or pick up the tab for coffee and dessert occasionally. Later, when you are asked to mentor someone, remember how it felt to be mentored without the restriction of cost.

As a mentor to working interpreters just out of an IPP but not yet certified, I discovered that the thing most people needed was guidance. During the first meeting, the following questions should be asked:

What are your goals for the mentorship?

What causes you problems during the task of transliterating?

What do you feel needs to be worked on?

Are these conclusions self-assessed, from another interpreter, or from a Deaf consumer?

What do you consider your weak areas? Your strong areas?

As you can see, a lot of questions are asked during the mentorship process, and through the answers, the mentor guides the person to self-awareness of the areas that need to be worked on. When you are stumped, your mentor can offer suggestions and give guidance. In the ensuing meetings, work on improving your skills based on the information learned in the first meeting. Perhaps you do not want to work with a mentor. There are other options, such as working with a partner.

Working with a Partner

Find someone who wants to work on transliterating skills as much as you do and ask to become transliterating partners. Set up weekly practice sessions to work on your skills and bring to the practice sessions any text you have found difficult. Texts can include books from classes you are working in, handouts received during assignments, outlines for future work, audio or videotapes, or any other interesting materials you want to work on. You can also seek out opportunities through an agency or place of employment where the two of you can work together.

Your partner should be aware of your goals and what skills you are developing and you should know theirs. You can come up with your own list of goals before you meet, or wait and work together on your goals. Decide in advance how long you want to work in one session. This could be one to one-and-a-half hours. Bring paper and pencils to write down points you want to remember.

Once you begin working together, each of you should feel free to point out improvements as well as areas of weakness for each other. When you give feedback, below are some guidelines for you and your partner to follow:

1. Do not feel you are in competition with your partner. Each of you has strengths and weakness.

2. Before you give feedback, ask your partner how she felt about her performance. What did she feel she did the best? The worst?

3. Do not give your partner more than she can handle. If you overload her with feedback, she may be overwhelmed and stop listening.

4. When you give feedback, do not expect your partner to agree or disagree. You are giving your impressions; the person receiving the feedback does not have to respond.

5. Help explore ways in which your partner can improve by asking questions.

6. Show empathy for your partner's feelings. No one likes to hear that they made a mistake. Keep it light.

7. Be specific in your feedback. Don't say "I couldn't read your fingerspelling," but rather, "You are dropping the last letters of the words you are fingerspelling." The more specific you are, the easier it will be to work on improving the skill.

8. Focus on the transliterating, not the person doing the transliterating.

Using Videotapes

Many people say they hate to see themselves on videotape. But like it or not, only by videotaping and viewing yourself can you truly know how well you are transliterating and what your consumer sees.

If you are already working as a transliterator, perhaps you can get permission to videotape yourself during an assignment. This is, of course, easier in a school setting or location in which you work on a regular basis. If this is not possible, videotape yourself at home for about 10 minutes.

Once you have videotaped yourself, watch yourself **with the sound off**. Only by watching yourself with no auditory cues can you see yourself the same way your Deaf consumers see you. Also, problem areas tend to become more evident when you rely on visual cues only. Observe and critique the tape with your partner or mentor, giving yourself feedback and act as if you were giving feedback to another person.

Helpful Hints

Expose yourself to ASL. Watch how Deaf adults use ASL and examine its grammar. The better your knowledge of ASL, the better your transliteration. Watch other transliterators and note what they do during their work.

Start paying attention to the way English is used and notice the idiomatic phrasing used to express ideas. Get a dictionary and check out what words really mean. Increase your English vocabulary. Take an English class to gain a better understanding of English grammar. Explore the richness of English.

SUMMARY

The goal of transliterating is to remain both equivalently and structurally similar to the source language while providing a clear message in the target form. Transliterators include many features of ASL, not just English-like signing structure, and the meanings of words and phrases must be clear to transliterators before they can clearly transliterate the meaning. As a transliterator, you will be involved in a life-long process of learning and striving to continually improve your skills. While improving your skills, you will move through four levels of learning: unconscious incompetence, conscious incompetence, conscious competence, and unconscious competence.

To improve your skills as a transliterator, you need to set goals. Be specific about what you want to improve and then prioritize your goals. Writing down your goals will make you more committed, but do not try to change everything at once. Concentrate on one goal at a time.

Practice your new skills physically and mentally. Yes, work on your transliterating skills by actually doing the task, but also visualize how you would perform the task of transliterating. Take the time to analyze a text and think about how you should transliterate it.

Working alone can be difficult, so find a mentor or partner. A mentor can be either another transliterator or a Deaf consumer. Set a limit to how many times you will meet and for how long. Another avenue is to work with a transliterating partner. Find someone who also wants to work on his or her transliterating skills and set up weekly practice sessions. Your partner can point out areas of improvement as well as skills that need more work.

It is important to observe yourself in the same way as your Deaf consumers do. Videotape yourself and view it with the sound off. Look not only for areas of weakness, but also for areas of strength. Keep improving your ASL and your English skills. The more you understand ASL and English the better you will perform the task of transliterating.

Now it is time to put this book down and get to work. Good luck on your journey into the world of transliterating.

ACTIVITIES

Activity 11-1

Establishing transliterating goals.

Step 1. Videotape yourself for 10 minutes transliterating.

Step 2. Identify any consistent skill areas that need improvement.

Step 3. Of the skill areas listed, choose the two you feel are the most important to work on.

Step 4. Look at your videotape again and find examples of the areas you want to work on. Describe each skill area in as much detail as you can.

Step 5. For each area in which the transliterating process breaks down, come up with two concrete goals to work toward to strengthen them.

Step 6. Write these goals in a place where you can refer to them easily.

■■■ APPENDIX

Transliterating: How RID Defines It

WHAT IS TRANSLITERATION?

Many candidates for the RID Certificate of Transliteration (CT) examination have requested guidance in an effort to understand the goals of the English-to-sign portion of the exam.

Raters have reviewed the minimum standard, in addition to performances of passing and failing candidates, and have agreed upon the following description of rating criteria for the current performance evaluation for the CT.

The three broad categories that raters evaluate have been described: Grammar and Vocabulary, Processing, and Mouth Movement Patterns.

Grammar and Vocabulary

- Use of space for role taking (characterization).

- Use of space for subject-object agreement and verb inflections.

- Conceptually correct sign choices (based on meaning rather than form).

- Some amount of "initialization," but only to the extent that initialization is used by Deaf adults (not to the extent of Manual English Codes).

- The ability to produce English that is generally grammatically correct and clearly enunciated, with few annoying habits (such as "um," "er," "you know").

Processing

- Lexical to phrasal level of processing, e.g., ranges from "word meaning for word meaning" to "more than words, less than sentences."

- Some restructuring or paraphrasing for clearer conveyance of meaning.

- Some additions of ASL signs that enhance the clarity of the visual message (modals such as CAN, classifier constructions, indexing, and listing structures).

- Detailed English morphology (e.g., manual English coding of "ing," "ed," and the copula), which is conveyed on the mouth but not with manual signs.

Mouth Movement Patterns

Cohesive English sentences are visibly presented on the lips, either as exact words from the original text or as English paraphrasing of the original text.

Finally, overriding all of the above details is the requirement that the target message resulting from the transliteration remain true and accurate with regard to the source text.

There should be no substitutions (missing a concept from the original and replacing it with a different concept) and no significant omissions (all of the main points and nearly all of the supporting details of the source test should be reflected in the target text).

The spoken English message should be true to the original signed message, with relatively few omissions, substitutions, or other errors.

In order to gain further guidance, the RID raters recommend that candidates for testing read Elizabeth Winston's article (1989), "Transliteration: What's the Message?" The description of transliteration in this article has been determined to be an accurate description of the performance of a successful candidate for the CT performance examination.

■■ REFERENCES

Akamatsu, C. T., & Stewart, D. A. (1989). The role of fingerspelling in simultaneous communication. *Sign Language Studies*, 65:361-374.

American Heritage Dictionary (1999). Boston: Houghton, Mifflin.

Baker, C., & Cokely, D. (1980). *American Sign Language: A Student Text*. Silver Spring, MD: T.J. Publishers.

Baker-Shenk, C. (1987). Manually coded English. In: *Gallaudet Encyclopedia of Deaf People and Deafness, 2*. New York: McGraw-Hill.

Battison, R. (1978). *Lexical Borrowing in American Sign Language*. Silver Spring, MD: Linstock Press.

Bornstein, H. (1987). Signed English. In: *Gallaudet Encyclopedia of Deaf People and Deafness, 2*. New York: McGraw-Hill.

Bornstein, H., Hamilton, L., & Saulnier, K. (1983). *The Comprehensive Signed English Dictionary*. Washington, DC: Gallaudet University Press.

Boyles, A. (1996). Who eats whom? *Highlights for Children*, 51(3):8-9.

Bragg, B. (1989). A wake-up call for hearing signers. In: M. D. Garretson, Ed., *Communication Issues among Deaf People. Eyes, Hands and Voices: A Deaf American Monograph, 1990*. Silver Spring, MD: National Association of the Deaf.

Caccamise, F., J. Stangarone, M. Mitchell-Caccamise, E. Banner, (Eds.) (1980) RID Code of Ethics. In: Proceedings of the 1980 RID Convention. "A Century of Deaf Awareness." Silver Spring, MD: Registry of Interpreters for the Deaf.

Carroll, L. (1960). *Alice's Adventures in Wonderland*. New York: Signet Classic Printing.

Cassell, J., & McCaffrey, E. (1995). *Instructional Guide. ASL Grammatical Aspects: Comparative Translations*. Salem, OR: Sign Enhancers.

Clark, T. S. (1995). Mentorship: A sign of the times. Regional Interpreter Training Consortium. Stillwater, OK: National Clearinghouse of Rehabilitation Training Materials.

Colonomos, B. M. (1989). *Depth of Processing*. Riverdale, MD: The Bicultural Center.

Davis, J. (1989). Distinguishing language contact phenomena in ASL interpretation. In: C. Lucas, Ed., *The Sociolinguistics of The Deaf Community*. San Diego: Academic Press.

Fant, L. J., Jr. (1975). *AMESLAN: An Introduction to American Sign Language*. Northridge, CA: Joyce Motion Picture Co.

Frishberg, N. (1990). *Interpreting: An Introduction*. Silver Spring, MD: Registry of Interpreters for the Deaf.

Gordon, J. R. (1999). *Organizational Behavior: A Diagnostic Approach*. Upper Saddle River, NJ: Prentice Hall.

Graduate School (1998). Grammar and Usage Workshops, Workshops: "The Government's Trainer."

Gustason, G., Pfetzing, D., & Zawolkow, E. (1980). *Signing Exact English*. Los Alamitos, CA: Modern Signs Press.

Gustason, G., & Zawolkow, E. (1993). *Signing Exact English*. Los Alamitos, CA: Modern Signs Press.

Hodges, J. C., & Whitten, M. E. (1982). *Harbrace College Handbook*. New York: Harcourt Brace Jovanovich.

Humphrey, J. H., & Alcorn, B. J. (1995). *So You Want To Be an Interpreter?: An Introduction to Sign Language Interpreting*. Amarillo, TX: H & H Publishers.

Humphries, T., Padden, C., & O'Rourke, T. J. (1994). *A Basic Course in American Sign Language*. Silver Spring, MD: T.J. Publishers.

Ingram, R. M. (1974). A communication model of the interpreting process. *Journal of Rehabilitation of the Deaf*, 7:3-9.

Isenhath, J. (1990). *The Linguistics of American Sign Language*. Jefferson, NC: McFarland & Company.

Isham, B. (Winter 1983). Beyond the classroom: Self-directed growth for interpreters. *The Reflector*, 6:15-17.

Kannapell, B. (1989). Inside the Deaf community. In: S. Wilcox, Ed. *American Deaf Culture: An Anthology*. Silver Spring, MD: Linstock Press.

Kannapell, B. (1982). Inside the Deaf community. *The Deaf American*, 34(4):23-26.

Kelly, J. (1999). Transliterating: A curriculum for interpretation preparation programs. Unpublished paper.

Kelly, J. (1998). What are we becoming? *VIEWS*, 15(8):8.

Klima, E., & Bellugi, U. (1979). *The Signs of Language*. Cambridge, MA: Harvard University Press.

Lane, H., Hoffmeister, R., & Bahan, B. (1996). *A Journey into the Deaf World*. San Diego: DawnSign Press.

Larson, M. L. (1984). *Meaning-Based Translation: A Guide to Cross-Language Equivalence*. Lanham, MD: University Press of America.

Lawrence, S. (1995). Interpreter discourse: English to ASL expansion. In: E.A. Winston, Ed. *Proceedings of the 10th National Convention Conference of Interpreter Trainers*. (pp. 205-215). Charlotte, NC: Conference of Interpreter Trainers.

Marron, S. (1999). Comparing ASL and English features: Implications for voice interpreting. Torrance, CA: Regional Interpreter Training Consortium.

Mather, S. (1989). Visually oriented teaching strategies with Deaf preschool children. In: C. Lucas, Ed. *The Sociolinguistics of the Deaf Community.* San Diego: Academic Press.

Matthews, K. C. (September 1995). Report on the National Testing System. *VIEWS,* 12(8):8.

McCrum, R., William, C., & MacNeil, R. (1987). *The Story of English.* New York: Penguin Books.

McIntire, M., Ed. (1986). Task analysis of interpretation and response. In: *Proceedings from the Fifth National Conference of Interpreter Trainers Convention.* Silver Spring, MD: Registry of Interpreters for the Deaf Publications.

Meadow, K. (1977). Name signs as identity symbols in the Deaf community. *Sign Language Studies,*16:237-246.

Miller, G. R. (1972). *An Introduction to Speech Communication.* New York: Bobbs-Merrill Company.

Moores, D. (1977). Issues in the utilization of manual communication. *Proceedings of the National Symposium on Sign Language Research and Teaching.* Silver Spring, MD: National Association of the Deaf.

Morris, W., Ed. (1980). *The American Heritage Dictionary of the English Language.* Boston: Houghton Mifflin.

Neuman, S. (1981). *Sign Language Interpreting: A Basic Resource Book.* Silver Spring, MD: National Association of the Deaf.

O'Connor, J., & Seymour, J. (1990). *Introducing Neuro-Linguistic Programming: The New Psychology of Personal Excellence.* London: Hartnolls Limited.

Padden, C. (1998). The ASL lexicon. *Sign Language and Linguistics,* 1:35-53.

Padden, C. (1991). The acquisition of fingerspelling by Deaf children. In: P. Siple & S. Fischer, Eds. *Theoretical Issues in Sign Language Research, Psychology.* Chicago: University of Chicago Press.

Phillips, R. S., Ed. (1983). Periodic law. In: *Funk and Wagnalls New Encyclopedia.* (Vol. 20, p. 261). Dunn and Bradstreet.

Quigley, S. P., & Youngs, J. P. (1965). *Interpreting for Deaf People.* Washington, DC: Department of Health, Education, and Welfare.

Registry of Interpreters for the Deaf. (1993). Introduction to the National Testing System. In: *Generalist Certification Examination Information Bulletin.* Silver Spring, MD: Registry of Interpreters for the Deaf Publications.

Research and Training Center on Mental Health for Persons Who Are Hard of Hearing or Late Deafened. (1995). [brochure]. San Diego: California School of Professional Psychology.

Roy, C. B. 1980. *Developing Curriculm for Interpreter Training Programs in Vocational Education, Final Report (1979-1980)*. Austin, TX: Texas Education Agency.

RSA Federal Interpreter Training Center. (1995). Professional development endorsement system: A curriculum for training interpreters for the Deaf in educational and rehabilitation settings. September 1995. (No. CFDA 84.160A). Winsted, CT.

Siple, L. A. (1997). Historical development of the definition of transliteration. In: M. L. McIntire & S. Wilcox, Eds. *Journal of Interpretation* (pp. 77-100). Silver Spring, MD: RID Publications.

Siple, L. A. (1996). The use of addition in sign language transliteration. In: D. M. Jones, Ed. *Proceedings of the Eleventh National Convention of Conference of Interpreter Trainers*. Little Rock, AR: Conference of Interpreter Trainers.

Stedt, J ., & Moores, D. (1990). Manual codes on English and American Sign Language: An historical perspective and current realities. In: H. Bornstein, Ed. *Manual Communication: Implications for Education* (pp. 1-20). Washington, D.C.: Gallaudet University Press.

Supalla, S. (1992). *The Book of Name Signs: Naming in American Sign Language*. San Diego: DawnSign Press.

Viera, J. A. (2000). Transliteration: the consumer's perspective. In: Watson, D., Ed. *Journal of Interpretation* (pp. 83-98). Silver Spring, MD: RID Publications.

Warner, H. C. (1987). Rehabilitation: Administration. In: *Gallaudet Encyclopedia of Deaf People and Deafness, 3*. New York: McGraw-Hill.

Wells, Jim, (1983). Comprehension of Fingerspelled Words and Numbers Within Signed Messages: Skill Development and Excercises. In: Proceedings of the 1983 RID National Comvention. "Golden Opportunities in Interpreting." Silver Spring, MD: RID Publications.

Wilcox, S., & Wilcox, P. (1991). *Learning To See: American Sign Language as a Second Language*. Englewood Cliff, NJ: Regents/Prentice Hall.

Winston, E. A. (1989). Transliteration: What's the message? In: C. Lucas, Ed. *The Sociolinguistics of the Deaf Community*. San Diego: Academic Press.

Winston, E. (1996). Defining Interpretation and Transliteration. In: *VIEWS*, 13(5). Pg. 19. MD: RID Publications.

Woodward, J. (1987). Sign language continuum. In: *Gallaudet Encyclopedia of Deaf People and Deafness, 3*. New York: McGraw-Hill.

Zawolkow, E. (1978). Signing exact English: A skill improvement session. In: F. Caccamise, J. Stangarone, & M. Caccamise, Eds. *Proceedings of the 1978 Registry of Interpreters for the Deaf Convention*. Silver Spring, MD: Registry of Interpreters for the Deaf.

Zola, E. (1980). Opening session address: Growth. In: F. Caccamise, J. Stangarone, & M. Mitchell-Caccamise, Eds. *Proceedings of the 1980 RID Convention*. Silver Spring, MD: Registry of Interpreters for the Deaf.